Tony Crofts

QUAKER AUTHOR

THE RETURN OF THE WILD

The British countryside and the world-wide rural crisis

IRELAND:
61 Newtown Road,
Waterford

BRITAIN:
High Street,
Stonesfield,
Oxon OX7 2PU

Copyright   TONY CROFTS   1987

ISBN: 0 - 948728 - 11 - 6

20014645

333.7

Cover Drawing after Botticelli by Irene Wise.

Back Cover Photograph by courtesy of Oxfam.

Published By   THE FRIENDLY PRESS
                         61 Newtown Road
                         Waterford

Printed by   Litho Press
                         Roxboro Mews,
                         Midleton
                         Co. Cork.

Contents

Illustrations (in centre of book)

Abandoned Bronze Age farms on Dartmoor
Field Size change in Suffolk in the 17th and 18th centuries
Land prices 1790-1980
U.N. projections of urban population
Britain's timber potential
Worldwide Distribution of Land to Population

PREFACE

During the writing of this book I have been extremely fortunate in being involved in the work of RURAL, the Society for Responsible Use of Resources in Agriculture and on the Land, which has brought me in contact with most of the best minds in agriculture, conservation and land use thinking. It has also given me ready access to a great deal of data and information I could only otherwise have gathered by many more months of research.

However, I must make clear that the conclusions and recommendations made in this book are purely mine, and do not in any way represent the thinking of the members or body of RURAL. Any errors or imbecilities are my own entirely.

Personal thanks are due to a number of people: to Christopher and Bridget Hill, for helping me to see history in a meaningful perspective; to Oscar Colburn for the unfailing clarity of the thoughts he has expressed; to Professor David Harvey of Reading University Dept of Agricultural Economics, Bob Bunce of the Institute of Terrestrial Ecology and Lewis Jollans of the Centre for Agricultural Strategy for giving me privileged access to their fundamental work on the consequences of different land use policies. To Frank Raymond for comments that were both shrewd and sympathetic, and to Murray Carter, a quite exceptional farmer pioneering new strategies for making the most of ordinary land. To Mary Cherry for sharing her wisdom and experience both of British and world agriculture; to Kevin Watkins of the Catholic Institute for International Relations for his incisive and always informed comments and advice, to John Campbell, Chief executive of the Economic Forestry Group, for sharing his professional experience without thrusting his own opinions, and to Dr Peter Savill of the Oxford-University

Forestry Dept. To Geoffrey Masefield, one of the world authorities on farming systems, and economist-turned Community Relations specialist Kamala Hyder, whom I was once fortunate enough to have as a tutors; and to many people in Oxfam who freely shared information and their own constantly-developing thoughts with me.

I acknowledge with grateful thanks permission from the estate of the late Sonia Brownell Orwell and Secker & Warburg Ltd to quote from George Orwell's essay "The English People"; from Sidgwick & Jackson Ltd to quote from William Clark's "Cataclysm", and from the Pluto Press to reproduce John Agard's poem "My Telly", from Macmillan Gill Ltd for permission to quote from Alan Mathews' "The Common Agricultural Policy and the Less-developed Countries" and from the SCM Press Ltd for permission to use the table on world distribution of land to population from Tissa Balasuriya's "Planetary Theology".

Particular thanks to the librarians of the Oxford University Institute of Agricultural Economics and Departments of Forestry and Agricultural Science, Oxford Polytechnic, and the Reading University Institute of Agricultural History, for their unfailing courtesy and assistance in my raids upon their resources. The result is not perfect, but I hope it may help some people to make new connections, and see things in a different and clearer light.

Stonesfield, January 1987

FOREWORD

In Britain, environmentalists grieve over the death of orchids, butterflies and village schools. Elsewhere in the world, it is children who die, in their thousands.

There is a connection. Britain is a jewelled microcosm of the troubles of the world, which arise fundamentally from a steady trend towards concentration of economic power. It expresses itself in greater centralisation of government, procurement, and marketing, with takeovers increasing gigantism in international corporations - many of whom deploy larger budgets than governments.

The trend expresses itself physically in the dizzying growth of cities. By the year 2015, more than half the world's population will have become urbanised. With it, grow the demands of the urban sector on the rural, and those of the economically fortunate elite on the broad mass of people.

In agriculture, the same process is clearly visible: a move towards the Global Farm supplying the Global Supermarket involves the steady amalgamation and enlargement of land holdings. And as it moves forward, people are pressed into cities: either driven off the land, or drawn by the vision of 'the good life'. In the process, human communities are destroyed, and with them, the environment degraded.

In north-east Brazil, large landowners hire gunmen to drive peasant farmers off land they wish to ranch to produce at lower unit cost for export onto an over supplied world market - for their own profit, and to pay off loans to developed world banks - while the native population starves. The desperate dispossessed clear rain forest to obtain land to till, and the fragile soil, water supply and climatic order start to shift and collapse.

Thus we run their agriculture fast, and destroy their

environment for our own benefit: for we are the privileged elite in the international economic order.

These forces are visibly acting in this country too, although in rather more urbane garb: but today as agricultural surpluses begin to force down market prices, large numbers of family farms are facing crippling financial pressures. Those with capital and muscle to expand and intensify will survive, and in the process produce a simplified countryside with a narrower range of wildlife.

But we have already been through the industrialisation which some developing countries are just entering; and others may never achieve, and are now emerging into a post-industrial society. The wealthier section of our urban population is now beginning the move back out into the countryside, which may have to accommodate another 5 million people by the year 2020. To achieve this without severe environmental degradation will require clear-headed and daring planning. An attempt to petrify the status quo will not suffice.

Conservation, here as in less forgiving climates, must begin with a people-based countryside. Deliberate measures are needed to guarantee land, resources and infrastructure to the family farm, together with encouragement to a vigorous and multifarious rural economy - which then feeds vigour and health back into the national economy and the whole community. In old societies like ours, the established structure of landholding and control is disguised by social and cultural factors, above all, the class system; but it is just as much a block to fair provision of the means of life as in more lawless parts of the world: and while its dismantling can be achieved without revolution or violence, determined and clear-sighted legal and fiscal measures must be taken to that end if economic, social and environmental health are to be re-established.

This book is addressed to all concerned with either society or environment; on either a domestic or international scale. It sets out to give for the first time a perspective that clearly relates parochial concerns to world problems, and firmly identifies the British countryside as a part of lifeboat earth.

CHAPTER 1 THE LAND: USED, USED UP OR STERILISED?

Ye fields, ye scenes so dear to Lubin's eye,
Ye meadow-blooms, ye pasture-flowers, farewell!
Ye banish'd trees, ye make me deeply sigh --
Inclosure came, and all your glories fell:
E'en the old oak that crown'd yon rifled dell,
Whose age had made it sacred to view,
Not long was left his children's fate to tell;
Where ignorance and wealth their course pursue,
Each tree must tumble down - old "Lea-Close Oak," adieu!

John Clare (1793-1864)

Few of the changes we apprehend in this country's rural landscape are irreversible: many have occurred before and passed away. A study of field sizes in Suffolk over the last three centuries shows that in the 18th century, many were very nearly as large as today; only to be broken down again in the 19th into the smaller fields we like to think of as 'normal'. Modern fertilisers, pesticides and herbicides have allowed us to dispense with rotations - which were the only tool our grandfathers had for maintaining soil fertility, field cleanliness and crop health - and thus changed the patchwork of the countryside: but not changed its basic material or condition.

Even the parts cherished as true wildscape - the uplands of the South-western peninsula, for instance - are actually an impoverished semi-desert, created by our neolithic and bronze age ancestors using the same kind of processes of deforestation that we condemn in the developing world today.

The same processes of landscape change work in all countries, reaching equilibrium under steady conditions of

1

climate, human use and occupancy. When these conditions are disturbed, the landscape changes - rapidly under extremes of heat or rainfall, more slowly in temperate conditions. It would not be difficult to make the German Black Forest look like the Southern uplands of Scotland, or the reverse: and the interesting thing is that the change in either direction would be likely to create an equal furore. The 'natural' landscape is generally that which people have been used to for two or three generations.

But the forces which upset these equilibria, which lead to drastic, even catastrophic landscape change, have a historical momentum of their own. The process of change which they induce has reached different stages in different parts of the world: and the dominating factors in fixing the current stage in each location are the density of population and the degree to which the Western pattern of economic development - the Green Revolution, urbanisation and the cash economy - has been adopted. Indeed striking parallels can be drawn between situations in less densely-populated, still-developing countries and events well recorded in our own history when the population was smaller and the social development of the country was at an earlier stage.

And while even the larger detail changes in the land can be arrested, given sufficient will and expenditure, the broad onward movement of man's occupation and exploitation of the earth has the inevitability of a juggernaut; and carefully planting flowers along its way will do little to deflect it. To achieve any significant modification of that process calls for major political action - of the order of the reorganisation of the Chinese peasant economy - or a far profounder understanding and willingness to accept communal responsibility than we have so far seen in Great Britain. Landscape change, it has to be said, IS a political phenomenon, in the broadest and truest sense. And the best way to start a lasting change for the better is by consciousness-raising at a grassroots level, with no pre-conditions. All too often, change decreed from above, unless in response to popular demand, is not fulfilled, but just left on the starting blocks. There will be political change by all means: but starting with education to change demands and buying habits; and only afterwards consolidated into legislation.

To return to specific, parochial environmental concerns: while it is easy to compile crude once-for-all tallies of herb-rich grassland and hedgerow lost, a more sensitive survey of landscape change between 1978 and 1984 carried out by the Institute of Terrestrial Ecology on a representative set of sites in eleven regions shows that, for instance, 93 per cent of the land newly put to wheat in that cereal boom period was not newly-broken, but had previously been under annual crops or short-term grass leys. This is evidence of the normal flexibility of farm business management in response to short-term market stimuli; not a massive and permanent destruction of the environment. Similarly, even in the south-east where change has been greatest, only 1.1 percent of rough grazings were improved or upgraded in that period; and while improvement included draining in half of cases, the majority of wetland sites identified in 1978 had remained undrained. While 24,700 hectares of broadleafed woodland and scrub were removed or underplanted with conifers, 26,000 were newly planted: and the greater part of this new broadleaf planting took place in south and central England. Lines of broadleaves were planted in East Anglia at three times the rate in the central and south-western regions, four times that in West Wales, and eight or more times that in the North; while that region received half of the total number of young hedgerow trees for the whole of Great Britain. Clearly,the trend towards hedgerow grubbing has stopped and is now running backwards: indeed Suffolk County Council's Farm Conservation Officer reports that the greatest problem she is facing at present is landowners wanting to take up Forestry Commission grants for broadleaf planting on precisely the grass meadows the conservation authorities most want to preserve - probably in hope of income from pheasant shooting to replace a grazing use that has fallen out of the economic mix of enterprises. The same survey showed that while field boundary removal continued in all regions, the length of new boundaries established was twice that removed: and although three-quarters of this was wire fencing, it was often associated with agricultural improvement or forestry.

Now, it must be said that the value of the areas gained is not immediately equivalent to that of those lost. A 300-year-old hedge will be far more species-rich than one only 10 years old. One oak is ecologically worth as much as 200 small trees. But it appears that the basic message is now being taken in, that possibilities must be retained, or re-created, for such richness to continue or develop.

Significantly, the survey found that an average of 6,500 hectares a year of land had been lost to housing, most of it previously vacant, derelict or under pasture - frequently the state of land subject to planning blight. The most building had taken place in East Anglia and other regions within commuting distance of London. A further 9,300 kilometres of tarmac roads and tracks had been built. In the six years, the area of golf courses increased by 14,000 hectares, caravan sites by 3,800. Total losses of agricultural land in the areas monitored averaged around 14,000 hectares a year - 22 per cent of all farmland in 30 years. Nationally, this century 1 million hectares have disappeared under bricks, tarmac and concrete. Horses in 1984 numbered well over half a million - or nearly half the number in the days when the horse was the sole source of motive power on the land - and now occupy something like 15 per cent of all lowland grass.

From these figures, it begins to be apparent that the true threat is not that of intensive agriculture: that can be quite readily scaled down or its trend reversed in a short span of years. It is the hunger to possess and control land, which, because suppressed in the urban majority of the population here during two centuries of industrial revolution, is only now coming clearly into the open in a multitude of costumes: many of them more flavoured with greed and competition than the simple use which survival demands.

This same hunger is being increasingly frustrated, meanwhile, in developing countries by the same macro-economic forces. While the suffering in our society has been transferred to a smaller section of the inner-city population, in many Third World countries it is now being imposed, on a harrowing and obscene scale, on the former rural majority of the population: and in the process, major and possibly irreparable damage is being done to the fabric of the ecosphere. No deserts, and fewer soil-stripped and eroded hills are being created in Great Britain: but the processes at work are the same as those in Sub-Saharan Africa and the Amazon basin: and the remedies here as there are just as much those of justice and fair husbanding of the nation's resources.

This is what it is easy to lose sight of in our mellow, comforting landscape and our comparative economic privilege. That the sufferings even of the least fortunate Britons do not express themselves in slavery, genocide, child labour or prostitution is an expression simply of our good fortune in having got in first on the ladder of economic power: and our good fortune - including the comparatively unravaged beauty of our countryside -has its share of the responsibility to bear for the inhuman sufferings of other members of the world's population.

The process of land use follows a fairly clear pattern in all societies. Here, as elsewhere, it started as the opportunist use of the nomadic hunter-gatherer: passed on to a system of family or tribal bases with clearly-defined territories containing outlying seasonal camps for the grazing movements of transhumance; and finally developed into regular settlements with a clear system of arable farming. At this stage, as in tribal societies in many parts of the world, land was fundamentally held in common, and its use allocated according to need and generally-acknowledged right.

Invasions - first by the Romans, then the Saxons and finally the Normans - imposed the priority land control of a victorious elite on the existing loose structure: but in most cases it was more a grafting onto an existing system than a complete restructuring: and in practice the land needs of the general population were recognised and satisfied. Settlements continued to float, be newly created, abandoned or expanded according to the movements of life itself; and although squatters were discouraged by the administrators of established communities, each parish accepted the responsibility for its own poor. It was not until the beginnings of the enclosure movement that the more successful and powerful holders started to consolidate their hold upon the land: and this process was not completed for practically three centuries. Only at the end of the 18th century, as Britain moved into the heyday of the Industrial Revolution, did we reach the situation where the ownership and occupancy of virtually all land was fixed: there was none spare or available for the poor or propertyless to camp upon; and those who had been effectively excluded from holding any land had been forced into the rapidly-expanding cities.

A condensed form of this process has taken place in many Third World countries within the last century: with settler colonists invading, taking over the best land, excluding the indigenous population, organising land tenure for their own power and benefit; and then, at independence, handing over this new structure to an alliance between a native elite and the multinational companies. The exponential growth of cities, with a headlong accretion of shanty towns and squatter camps, are the direct expression of this minority seizure and alienation of popular land rights, the destruction of a communal possession of the land which provided for the needs of all; overlaid and assisted by the seductive attraction to the rural young of the cities' sophisticated facilities. Where the poor and dispossessed have remained outside the cities, their struggles to survive, excluded from the more fertile land, increasingly precipitate ecological and environmental disasters. The removal of land cover, soil erosion, drought, starvation and finally the refugee camps of those who can no longer feed themselves, are the other face of the coin of the camps on urban rubbish tips: and all are the direct relatives of the crime-infested warrens of Dickens' London, one tenth of whose population had to survive by prostitution.

Today, having got onto the conveyor-belt of industrialisation early and pressed half the world into our service as suppliers of raw materials and customers for our goods and technology - shackling them in the process to trading disadvantage, underdevelopment and technological dependence - the majority of our population have reached the level of economic independence where they are able to demand homes and security of their own. The habit of communal and co-operative holding of land has been completely replaced by individual possession: and that in turn has produced a drive by the formerly dispossessed to reoccupy land on a personal basis, even in small parcels.

Even the planning of public housing is carried out according to middle-class, property-developing ideals, which assume ideal solutions will involve wholesale demolition of inner-city housing, the removal of millions to new settlements in the country, or their stacking in tower blocks with "open space" around them. No understanding is shown of the basic human need to be able easily to survey a given territory: the supervision which, rather than ownership, is the essence of control; and because the land cleared by demolition is not recognised as the communal cultural property of those who lived on it, but only valued in speculative terms of its development value, the whole cycle is given another upwards twist.

It manifests itself in an outward pressure of urban-style land use and valuation whose appetite for the countryside expressed itself grossly in the suburban sprawl of the 1930s, but is present in just as real a way in the gentrification of country cottages by commuters today. That urban membrane spreads outwards wherever it is allowed, and in the process stretches itself so thin at the centre that holes begin to appear in it. And at the perimeter, although still quite transparent, it expresses itself in conflict with the traditional rural land uses, decrying or suspecting agriculture more out of envy than understanding. The conflict is the most bitter where the farmers have also adopted the same standards of valuing land as capital, rather than as space for human life and work. And the urban outcomers, with rich inconsistency, condemn the farmer for doing as they themselves do.

Even on the husbandry front, the very high-tech mass-agricultural solutions that are hailed as the "Green Revolution" for developing countries, we deplore when our own farmers practise them. And while we patronisingly offer the surplus production of our own over-developed agriculture as a solution to the sufferings of their dispossessed - thus neatly perpetuating our own view of them as incapable and dependent - we are not yet ready to pay out of our affluence for our depredations on their economies and agriculture. When these liabilities come home to us in the form of subsidy bills to market unwanted produce, or storage costs for market intervention stocks, we turn upon our own landholders, reject and blame them, although they are simply the rural facet of our own greed. It produces a lopsily partial, wilfully blind argument. And yet books have been written and sold upon it, and a one-eyed view has gained wide currency.

In truth, a great deal of conservation thinking is basically a fear of and resistance to change, wanting not to face these very consequences of our own way of living. A wish to arrest time in a freeze frame from just before the Industrial Revolution, without having to forgo the material benefits of industry. It values one specific mode of rural organisation more than any others - either before or since - and wilfully ignores that that mode is no longer viable under the present economic order; nor would anyone be willing to pay its cost. More important than this fairly harmless nostalgia, it denies to the countryside the vital functions of life, which are the cycle of birth, growth, degeneration, death and rebirth. And, in selecting the wrong enemy, and laying its fearful hand to hold the countryside still, it itself imposes an urban concept of life upon the rural, and thus covertly advances the very disease it fears.

CHAPTER 2 FREE TRADE AND THE ECONOMIC TRAP

The proposition has been long and trenchantly argued that grants, subsidies and guaranteed high prices for farm produce have led British agriculture into an orgy of production on land over half of which is unsuitable. In the process, it is said, grave and wanton damage has been done to our own environment, and resources have been sucked in and consumed which would better have been spent building up food production in developing countries with no alternative option for economic activity, but more promising soils and climates.

At the same time, this artificial activity has inflated land values far above their true economic level, monopolising capital which could have been used to renew and invigorate our manufacturing industry, distorting and weakening our entire economy.

If only, it has been said, Britain could go back to free trade, buying her food wherever in the world it was to be most cheaply found, our cost of living would be reduced, we should stop loading our surpluses onto the world market and fatally depressing it for those whose only livelihood is to be gained from producing food and primary commodities. Further, such a regime would re-expose our agriculture to reality, and allow it to go back to doing what it does best - extensive livestock production by many small farmers. Land values would sink to their natural level, and entry to farming become open to young and vigorous entrepreneurs at present obliged to wait helplessly at the bottom of a ladder with most of the lower rungs missing.

These arguments have been seized on, and half digested, by the media and a range of special interest groups, and then used as a stick to beat farmers. A remarkable transformation has been wrought in public perception. From John Bull, sturdy yeoman, patriot and guardian of the countryside, the farmer's image has been transformed, in the space of little more than a decade, into greedy entrepreneur, tax sponger and destroyer of the environment. And the farmer himself, who is in truth no more venial than any other member of the population, is left bewildered and marginalised.

The current picture is no more accurate a representation of reality than the romantic fantasy it replaced; and while it claims to be supported by convincing economic, environmental and political arguments, the level on which these are deployed almost guarantees that they are accepted in terms of prejudice rather than understanding.

In the process, we lose sight of the complex and fragile structure of the countryside and the rural economy, and fail even to catch a glimpse of our own position in the world economy. Panaceas are peddled which appeal to fears and hungers which have never been fully diagnosed: panaceas which, if recklessly applied, could precipitate damage far greater than that already apprehended. There is a considerable risk of the baby's being thrown out with the bathwater.

It may well be that the picture of the grasping, threatening, exploitative farmer currently liked by the media and satirists is in fact a reflection of more general anxieties: a compound of envy, longing for security and a vague general feeling that something is amiss. The suspicion that someone is doing better than us, probably at our expense, and that we are in danger of losing our birthright, health and innocence, is understandable in a world where steady employment, economic stability and national security all appear threatened by forces almost beyond our comprehension and certainly beyond our control.

By the process known to psychologists as "displacement", a fear of the bomb or of unemployment become substituted by an obsession with fats, dangerous additives or agrochemicals Table salt and potash mechanically extracted from underground layers deposited by the drying up of primeval seas, or phosphate which has been washed out of the land into the seas and then cycled through plankton, fish and seabirds to end up as mineable rock guano, are branded 'chemicals', while salt freshly dried from the ocean, or potash and phosphate contained in recent animal manures are regarded as non-noxious: when in truth it is not the materials themselves, but the economic pressures which lead to their over-use, which are dangerous.

Further, these economic pressures are all simplified and ascribed to the farmer's greed, so that the 'threat' can be identified and personified: which removes the need to recognise that they actually arise from a complicated historical mixture of the role land ownership has played in our society, wartime patriotism, postwar egalitarianism and a political drive to ensure European self-sufficiency and prevent intra-European conflict; and a system of land tenure that has strayed far from the communal holding of land which followed the first steps from nomadic pastoralism to settled agriculture. All these factors have compounded with the demands expressed in the market place by the urban population - including precisely those critics - for low-priced, safe food of high quality, mainly from multi-outlet grocery chains: demands which can only be met by modern "intensive" production systems.

The burden of this book is that the issues are far more complex than is generally allowed. The motives which drive the argument are deep, powerful, and only partly-acknowledged; the true dangers are in many ways others than those most loudly-proclaimed; and the factors restraining our ability to avoid them, far more severely limiting than most of us would like to believe.

It is precisely because the arguments have generally been presented in simplistic terms, taking into consideration only an emotional concern, a social, aesthetic or political ideal or a "nothing-but" economic analysis, that the discussion has not advanced very far beyond accusation and assertion. Or, where they have been particularly emphatic, or have touched a raw nerve in the public mind, they have opened the door to poorly-planned, inadequately thought-through, frequently destructive measures. A patient for whom amputation is prescribed will have to devise a wooden leg, a crutch or a trolley to get around on: in a sane society, the surgeon is teamed with experts in artificial limb design and fitting. But where the patient is the land we live in, many feel free to call for drastic measures without giving any systematic thought to the function fulfilled by the things they propose dispensing with, or what will take their place.

The land is a national asset, and as such has a dual function. To the countrydweller, it is a workplace, livelihood and source of food production. That function has become inextricably confused with investment, property values and capital growth. To the towndweller, it is a fundamental source of spiritual and cultural nourishment - a demand that has been amplified by the great growth of mobility in this century which for the first time permits a mass of the population to visit the countryside. This expresses itself in a range of responses from wanting to tell the farmer how to do his job and restrict his freedom to do it to a far greater degree than any urban worker would accept, to the anarchy of mass trespass and animal liberation terrorism.

The former process has saddled agriculture with a fixed cost which has distorted its whole economy, and may end by depriving some farmers of the land they at present work, through bankruptcy; the latter seems quite likely to produce a major challenge to the traditional rights of property ownership. Both, it will be noticed, boil down to the same thing: the question of who owns and uses the land, and how that use and ownership is to be regulated.

The situation has come under a spotlight because of the increase in farm production achieved in the past 40 years. In that time, farming has been transfrmed from a largely craft industry to a highly intensive technology-based one. It is a process in which some other members of the Common Market are still following us, some way behind. The potential for further expansion of the EEC surpluses, as Greece, Spain, Portugal, and the bottom end of French farming catch up, is huge. Nor is it realistic to expect them to forgo the advantages of technical advance which we have already reaped.

The free trade option is not going to help this. In the past, a cheap food policy has gone hand in hand with industrial expansion, or at least buoyancy. Its effect has been to release labour from the unprofitable section of agriculture to supply the needs of manufacturing. Today, not only is the trend in industry irreversibly in the direction of more capital- and less labour-intensiveness; but the decay of our industrial base is in any case so far advanced that possibly our only hope of reconstruction lies in the support to be derived from EEC membership.

Nor, in the gathering momentum of international economic organisation, is it conceivable that we could survive slipping the link with the European market. It may be that our only role is as a foothold in Europe for US and Japanese multinationals: it is mere delusion to imagine our mounting our own independent challenge.

In any case, free trade is unlikely to be helpful to the cause of conservation. Agriculture, too, has gone a long way down the road of labour-shedding and capital-intensification. It has been said that "one man's wages will buy an awful lot of herbicide". Exposure to 'market forces' is likely in many areas to exacerbate precisely the effects of which environmentalists complain, as farmers struggle to keep afloat by increasing productivity. It has already happened. If 1971 farm sales, in real money terms, are taken as 100, those of 1985 register as only 80. Already in the 1986 harvest, the area grown to wheat - which produces a greater bulk of yield, but more often only of animal feed quality - is for the first time greater than that of barley. And the proportion of spring barley - which is normally of higher quality, and requires fewer sprays because of the sanitary break overwinter - to winter barley, which gives a heavier yield, has fallen. In a desperate situation, farmers are going for quantity, not quality.

More generally, in the nine years starting in 1976, the UK dairy industry increased its output by 20 per cent even as the real price of milk went down by the same amount; while cereal output doubled as cereal prices declined by 26 per cent. As prices were further forced down, we should be likely to move towards a countryside made up of large-scale arable farms and intensive livestock units interspersed with Sites of Special Scientific or Scenic Interest. The family farmer with one worker would either have to enlarge, or revert to own labour only - a serious regression if farming livestock. Official Annual Reviews of Agriculture show this polarisation in farm size to be taking place.

Where more extensive farming is the strategy chosen to cope with lower market prices, it will normally be conducted on larger farms: so that production is gathered more thinly from a larger area to yield the same end income. The Institute of Terrestrial Ecology's Merlewood station in Cumbria has monitored change in its own valley: where 216 farms have been regrouped into 76 in the past three decades. The trend towards farm amalgamation is almost certainly historically irreversible. It is proceeding, some way behind us, but at a gathering rate, in other European countries; and as steps are taken to control surpluses by more realistic pricing, can only be reinforced.

There are only two things which could change that fact. One is legislation stringently controlling the amount of land which may be held under one ownership: and while that exists and operates in other countries with a more republican history than ours, in Britain it would be reversing 300 years of trend and centuries of tradition. In any case, the size limit would certainly be set well above the present average farm size. Even the most enthusiastic proponents of farm size control have settled on the size where economies of scale cease to operate (between 125 and 166 hectares/300-400 acres), which is more than double the existing average of 64 hectares/154 acres.

Ironically, it is in the areas which are still closest to the conservationist's ideal that the greatest damage is likely to be done by the cold wind of economic reality. "Traditionally-run farmsteads, mostly small in size, where there are insufficient resources to create change or induce innovation, are some of those likely to display environmental health," said Professor Timothy O'Riordan of the University of East Anglia's School of Environmental Sciences at a recent high-level closed seminar on farm structure. But they are "at best only marginally viable and likely to become bankrupt as agricultural enterprises." That is why the only other possible brake on farm amalgamation may be a forthright acceptance by government that it is right and necessary to give direct income support to non-viable farms for social or landscape reasons.

It is clear - indeed it has been demonstrated in the past - that a policy of economic rigour towards agriculture rapidly results in a degraded environment. In the 1930s, the hedges met in the middle of the fields on the heavy land now used by the Ministry of Agriculture's Drayton Experimental Husbandry Farm near Stratford-upon-Avon. Any plan seriously to cut back or limit agricultural output will have to have built into it substitute uses or supports not only for the land but also for the rural population dependent on it. The mere removal or reduction of existing supports will only ensure that the most economically efficient survive and become redder in tooth and claw. The rest will either go to the wall and be swallowed up, or will adjust to a lower level of existence. British farming has an enormous capacity to tighten the belt, patch, make do and mend.

The consequences of that adjustment are unlikely to be very pretty. The level of inputs used on the best land is likely to rise, while that on the poorer land will tend to be cut, producing a partly-farmed countryside split between two environmentally undesirable sectors. Lower-input farming, far from being more 'natural', may well prove to be careless farming, as former Ministry of Agriculture Chief Scientists Frank Raymond has pointed out. Cheaper, wide-spectrum chemicals may be used rather than more expensive ones which are more selective in their action; spray application may be done with less control, with 80 per cent or more of the chemical going elsewhere than on the crop, because precise and well-maintained machinery costs more; poorly-maintained, sub-standard buidlings may become more common, walls less well-maintained. Indeed, while possibly better from the point of view of animal welfare and soil condition, the current proliferation of outdoor pig arks can hardly be said to have done much to enhance the landscape of the chalk downlands. At the marginal fringe, the withdrawal from upland areas which can be seen to have occurred several times before in history, would take place again, leaving dereliction rather than true wilderness behind it.

It is high time that we recognised that it is essential to de-link farming and countryside use from crude market economics: to set ourselves free to make a rational assessment of what we require of it, and construct a rational economic organisation to make it possible.

In fact, the direction of current thinking and EEC policy seems to be firming towards support for the small family farm on social or environmental grounds. The large question is what will be done eventually to reduce or eliminate the costly surpluses produced by those of the middle rank. On a crude analysis, forecasts are being made of over 1.6 million hectares/4 million acres being surplus to our requirements by the end of the century. The steady 2.5 per cent per year advance in cereal and dairy cow yields are estimated nearly to halve the area that will be required to produce 1985's needs in 2015.

It is important that we do not rush back into a situation like that just before the last war, when it was only the numbers - rumoured to have been as high as 70 per cent - of farmers who were technically insolvent - that kept the banks from foreclosing. Already, farming is facing a situation akin to the Depression of the 1930s. While prices were held at high levels by the EEC, costs, particularly the cost of land, rose to meet them. Now, as prices are pushed down, the falling returns from farming depress land values and threaten the liquidity of a significant number of farms. In late spring 1986, the Agricultural Director of one of the big clearing banks stated on the radio that he expected to see some 10,000 farms go out of business in the next few years. Not all would become bankrupt, he said: but many would have to sell up. It would be easy, at this time, to flip farming into a depression from which only a very long and painful haul, or very intensive measures (like those at the outbreak of war) could rescue it.

For instance, farmer and broadcaster Dan Cherrington, has already publicly foreseen a large part of the South Downs going out of all production very quickly if measures to cut the cereal surplus are applied "brutally enough to start working." This traditional sheep land could not stand the competition if other, more prosperous land, forced out of cereals, turned to intensive sheep production on a non-pastoral system. The alternative avenue of dairying, closed by quotas, or other extensive livestock farming, showing weaker returns, will not be available.

This brings us onto the other threat, whose consequences in the lowlands are far harder to undo. It bears remembering that the 1930s were the last time that agricultural land prices were low: and the immediate result, even in the general economic depression, was a huge increase in urban demand for land. The suburbs spread outwards in an uncontrolled tide, in ribbons along the highways. The resulting loss of countryside was so catastrophic that the 1947 Town and Country Planning Act was brought in to prevent its ever happening again. Already today, the house building industry is increasing its pressure on local authorities to relax their control of Green belts, proposing new "village communities" to be built on what is now farmland. Under a Conservative government, there has already been one hint of a willingness to treat Green belts more freely - stopped initially by a back-bench revolt of MPs with rural constituencies. But it is a straw in the wind.

In fact, what may prevent our seeing large areas of derelict farmland in the south-east, above all else, is the much higher level of wealth and incentive in some other parts of the economy. But this same wealth represents another powerful influence bearing on the future of the countryside. The urban demand for recreation and property in the country has for the first time become a major factor in the equation. Combined with the weakening of agriculture's economic strength, it makes the situation of the countryside unprecedentedly fluid.

At the same time, it is perfectly true we can no longer rely on living in a surplus economy, with farm incomes guaranteed by artificially high prices for the food they produce. This is a kind of phoney respectability, a pretence that our farmers are actually earning their living in the market: when in fact the whole thing is a theatrical exercise in a rigged situation. Our own consumers and taxpayers may squawk at having to pay some part of the costs of keeping this theatre open: but this is the complaint of the already-privileged. In any rational scenario, they will have - and be well able - to carry the cost of the countryside which they themselves cherish and use. The real crime is that the whole structure depends on other parts of the world's continuing to accept the unacceptable: the burden of both feeding and absorbing our surpluses. We cannot go on creating new Ethiopias to act as our final Intervention stores.

It is true that the present world food surplus may be at least partly due to economic recession and the inability of many countries to purchase imports of food. True, also, that at present consumption levels and on present trends of population increase, world demand for cereals could be an additional 120 million tonnes by the year 2000. However, the pace of technical advance, particularly with the new biotechnologies shortly promising greater pest, disease and weed control, higher quality and improved plant efficiency, seems likely to keep up with that demand. In any case, food need can only become demand by surplus income becoming available to purchase food: and that is likely to remain a serious block, particularly in Africa. Even where effective demand exists, it is unsafe to assume that the EEC will succeed in capturing it in a trade war such as is already looming with America's desperate and mighty agricultural sector.

Moreover, the economic and political impact of the developed on the developing world is not restricted to food trade. Seventy-seven per cent of British arms exports are to the Third World: and each warplane, missile or armoured vehicle sale hailed as guaranteeing a few more British jobs is quite likely to be used in a conflict that drives more peasants to flee the land they need to cultivate. The current starvation in the horn of Africa is far more the product of civil war stoked by arms supplies from big power sponsors, than of drought or natural disaster.

Even where the influence appears beneficent, it often works to increase the disadvantage of the less-developed country. The situation of Nigeria is instructive. In the 1970s, during the era of high oil prices, that country embarked on a huge oil-financed public infrastructure investment. Predictably, this resulted in a mass influx of population from the rural areas into the towns, seeking the new prosperity to be gained from urban life and work. The agricultural sector accordingly decayed. Food prices, however, were not allowed to rise as home-produced supplies fell off, because the government imported cheap surplus wheat (mainly from the USA -but the actual developed world source is irrelevant to the point in question) and sold it at controlled prices in Lagos. This prevented the rise of unrest in the new urban lower middle class, by teaching them to eat bread. It led both to the development of a new, wheat and bread-based food industry, and the the further undermining of traditional local foodgrain production, mainly sorghum and millet.

Expensively-financed development projects to increase self-sufficiency by boosting home production of wheat served further to entrench the position of this new food industry, but proved agronomic failures. Then, when the oil boom collapsed, the country suddenly became unable to finance continued economic development, leaving itself facing a serious crisis with a seriously-weakened agricultural sector. However, it was still obliged to maintain wheat imports at the same level, taking up an increasing share of its available foreign exchange, to prevent price rises and bread shortages which would cause unrest in the more volatile and politically-organised urban population.

Thus developing countries are pressed into supporting and financing the prettiness of our countryside and our affluence, and increasingly pay the price. As they become less able to continue that support as paying consumers, the world market weakens. Reverting to free trade, unleashing our buying power on that market - on which many of them now depend - will only force prices up and increase their disadvantage; even while also weakening our baseline agriculture. Unless alternative, realistic economic supports for the British countryside are found, it will begin having to put on threadbare clothes in some parts, succumb to urbanisation in others. The relentless advance of bracken over the uplands and the remorseless growth of spec-built housing estates around towns both feed on the weakness and oversimplification of agriculture.

The actual dangers facing us are insidious but unspectacular. If they are not recognised and provided against, a withering not just of our agriculture but of our countryside itself will take place. Inevitably, intensive arable production will continue in almost any foreseeable conditions on islands of the best land. But the rest will suffer a slow trivialisation or suburbanisation in some areas, an increase in unkemptness in others as capital investment is postponed or foregone, and the more labour-intensive aspects of management shelved.

The Return of the Wild is something which exists both in rural possibility and in the urban mind. At worst, it may take the form of an increase in scrub and dereliction: at best a strengthening of the landscape character of the country. Somewhere in between these two is a mild degradation of the landscape under continuing but half-cock use, which would guarantee that whatever our economic status, we have a second-rate countryside. And this visible malaise, like a skin eruption, will be symptomatic of the overall disease of the world economic/environmental order. If we treat our own symptoms only with local remedies, rather than remedying the deep-rooted misorganisation that produces them, that disease will continue on its cancerous way, throwing up ever grosser ills as it goes.

CHAPTER 3 THE PURSUIT OF PRIVILEGE

"The ambition to be a country gentleman, to own and administer land and draw at least a part of your income from rent, has survived every change.

The basic reason for this may perhaps be that England is very small; and has an equable climate and pleasantly-varied scenery. It is almost impossible in England, and not easy even in Scotland, to be more than twenty miles from a town. Rural life is inherently less boorish than it is in bigger countries with colder winters. And the comparative integrity of the British ruling class - for when all is said and done they have not behaved so contemptibly as their European opposite numbers - is probably bound up with their idea of themselves as feudal landowners.

This outlook is shared by considerable sections of the middle class. Nearly everyone who can afford to do so sets up as a country gentleman, or at least makes some effort in that direction. The manor house with its park and its walled gardens reappears in reduced form in the stockbroker's weekend cottage, in the suburban villa with its lawn and herbaceous border, perhaps even in the potted nasturtiums on the window-sill of the Bayswater flat. This widespread daydream is undoubtedly snobbish, it has tended to stabilise class distinctions: but it is mixed up with a kind of idealism, a feeling that style and tradition are more important than money."

George Orwell: The English people.

In his book "Agriculture: the Triumph and the Shame", Richard Body blamed the rise in land values during the 1970s on the high returns guaranteed to agriculture by government and EEC policies. It was an easy Aunt Sally to put up, and rapidly became a popular target for many sections of the non-farming population. But it depends on a gross oversimplification, and on completely ignoring the fundamental historical and political role played in our society by land ownership. Land values have been climbing steadily ever since the bottom of the great Depression in 1930; indeed, if you discount the effect of poor harvests in the late 19th century, World War I and the Depression, they are today about on target for the rate of climb started in the 1820s, when the Industrial Revolution was coming into its heyday.

In any case, there are other enterprises with very comparable trading situations and a not dissimilar cost structure to farming. If it were simply a guaranteed market and guaranteed prices that have led to this development in Britain, the same phenomenon would be as exaggerated in the other member states of the EEC. And it is not. In many European countries, land prices have remained substantially lower than ours; and in none has their rise been associated with such a marked run-down of industrial strength.

No, there is something special about the English appetite for land ownership, which explains and nourishes the innate and enduring conservatism of our society, and is inextricably involved with the so-called "British disease" which is manifesting itself in the later stages of economic decline. The preference for making money rather than things, for investing in capital growth rather than manufacturing capacity or genuine wealth creation, goes hand in hand with an exaggerated respect for collateral security. This in turn characterises the approach of our banking system to enterprise,and the timidity and sluggishness of much of our industrial management.

In terms of the best indices of economic health, investment in research and development and industrial renewal, the only European countries which now rank lower than Britain are Greece and Portugal. Before everything, I would argue, this is due to the role that ownership of property, and the status that is acccorded to it, have come to play in Britain. To justify this assertion, it will be necessary briefly to review the history and development of land use and tenure in this country.

The gradual colonisation and opening-up of England and Wales after the departure of the Romans had led to the establishment of a large part of the villages and towns we know today, by the time of the Norman Conquest. Some of these were hamlets in the depths of woodland with a few small, hard-won, irregular-shaped fields that were walled or hedged as they were cleared from the forest. Others were fully-formed nucleated villages with the typical open fields of feudal and medieval times. The shapes of these two types of original fields can still clearly be seen in the landscape; and the ridge and furrow formed by the two-way ploughing of the Saxons, which threw soil up towards the centre of each family's strip, is still striking in many parts of the Midlands.

On this fairly equal sharing of the land resources, was imposed the structure of the Norman baronies and the invader's monarchy. Large tracts of land were marked out as Royal forests - which meant more in terms of hunting rights than density of tree cover, for the clearance of the primeval forests was already substantially completed in Saxon times, and the attack on the moorlands had already begun.

Saxon kings had had their parks for hunting, but the Normans extended their 'forest law' over large tracts of already-cultivated land so that by the time of Henry II it may have covered as much as a third of the whole country. "The whole of Essex lay under forest law, and the whole of the Midlands from Stamford bridge in Lincolnshire south-westwards to Oxford bridge, a distance of eighty miles. By the thirteenth century a great belt of forest extended from the Thames at Windsor through Berkshire and Hampshire to the south coast" says Hoskins in The Making of the English Landscape. The creation of the New Forest actually destroyed numerous pre-existent villages.

The determination of the medieval peasant farmers to be free of this kind of imposition expressed itself in a willingness to pay substantial fines for making assarts (clearances) in the Royal forest, and in time to subscribe large sums to the Exchequer to have their country 'disafforested'. Both Richard I and John used this as a means of raising revenue, and the men of Devonshire, for instance, paid no less than five thousand marks - the equivalent of well over a million pounds today - in 1204 to have the whole of their county freed.

At the same time, the right to vote had been tied to property ownership, even in towns, where it was accorded only to the 10 freeholders, which identified land and political power. In the 12 and 13th centuries there followed a positive fever of borough creation as people scrambled for status and the power to administer their communities as they wished.

The great monastic houses forcibly depopulated quite large areas, destroying villages to create large enclosed granges for sheep farming in the 12th and 13th centuries; and this process was continued by secular landlords during the decline of population and economy stemming from the Black Death. Enclosure was already well advanced in some regions by the time of Elizabeth I.

The landowners, together with the Church - whose local priest's living lay in their gift - were also Justices of the Peace. Their first concern was to prevent any homeless poor from settling in their villages and becoming a charge on the parish; but a secondary one was to challenge and erode the customary rights of small tenants and copyholders to squat, build, and pasture stock on the land they occupied. In the process of agreed rationalisations of land holdings, the rights of subsistence farmers were taken away, and the beginnings of the migration into towns brought about, in a process that can today be seen going on in many developing countries. (Capitalistic agriculture for profit actually diminishes the ability of the population at large to feed itself, and makes it dependent on those who hold the monopoly of farmland and the ability to produce food.)

In particular, in Kent, Essex and Devon, where some of the original fields were still as first won from the forest, and there was no shortage of pasture so that the yeomen farmers had less need jealously to guard their rights of pasture over arable following harvest, the pooling of arable strips to create larger, enclosed grazing fields, was largely complete by the time of Good Queen Bess. Another motive encouraging the consolidation of holdings by purchase and exchange, followed by the erection of coppice fences, may have been to make good the loss of fuel resulting from forest clearance. In some parts of England, woodland cover was already so sparse that by the 17th century there was a famine of timber supplies for fencing, building and fuel.

Elsewhere in the country, Parliament had acted as a brake on the process. In a fascinating case quoted by Hoskins, a squire named John Spencer, who had bought the manor of Wormleighton on the borders of Warwickshire and Northamptonshire from William Cope, cofferer to the Household of Henry VII, was arraigned before Cardinal Wolsey's commission of enquiry into depopulating enclosures.

Eight years before the sale, Cope had evicted the occupiers of twelve farms and three cottages - some 60 people in all - and enclosed 240 acres of arable with hedges and ditches to convert them into sheep and cattle pastures. (It is an interesting fact that always, in times of economic distress, the balance tends to swing away from arable towards livestock farming - a point to which I shall return.)

The commission ordered Spencer to pull down the new hedges and restore the lands to tillage. The points he cites in his defence petition are striking: that he had built and maintained thr church and bought all its ornaments, cross, books, cope, vestments, chalice and censers, and maintained a full-time priest; that he had built four houses as well as his own; that he had set trees and sown acorns for timber and wood, double ditched and set with all manner of wood both in the hedgerows and also between them, "which is already grown to the profit of all them that should dwell in the said lordship". He also pleaded that he had no other pasture left him now in his country but this, "which if now put in tillage ... it shall be to his utter undoing, for his living is by the breed of cattle in his pastures, sold ... when fat to the city of London." A good landlord, a good conservationist, an admirable farmer, and ill able to afford bureaucratic interference in his management of his own land. And no doubt one who would feel quite at ease in the modern Country Landowners' Association.

But the most interesting aspect of this case is that, despite being ordered in 1522 to destroy all the hedges and ditches and restore all the lands to tillage by Candlemas, and further to rebuild all the houses demolished by their predecessor, the

Spencers managed to avoid ruin, and indeed acquired more land in the pastoral uplands of Northamptonshire and installed themselves at Althorp, when they founded two noble families - the Earls Spencer of Althorp (the family of the present Princess of Wales) and the Spencer-Churchills who subsequently became the Dukes of Marlborough. It shows the remarkable resilience of the hold on land and property of a social class.

But it was not until after the Civil War and the Restoration that the Enclosure movement really began to go forward with its full momentum. Until 1646, all landlords had technically been tenants of the Crown, and, in the frequent event of the occupant's dying before his heir had reached the age of 21, the Court of Wards would install someone to administer the estate until the heir reached his majority. Often, this would be some courtier seeking favours, who merely exploited the land and ran it down while he had the benefit of it. The King finally conceded the abolition of this system three years before his execution: and the first act of the landed gentry on inviting his son to resume the throne, was to ensure that it was not revived. For the first time, they had the security of freehold tenure, and longer-term agricultural improvement became worthwhile, unthreatened by an unpredictable wardship.

Following the devastation of the Plague, "England was filling up with people, recovering vigorously from the long decline of late medieval times; the towns were growing quickly, London above all, and constituted a large food market; industries were growing and needed in ever-increasing quantities of such country products as leather and wool. Farmers had an assured market at prices that were rising from the 1540s onwards." The great age of country house building that produced Montacute, Compton Wynyates, Longleat and Woburn began in Shakespeare's time, but it was only with the stability of the re-establishement of the monarchy that the consolidation of land holding spread to take in the whole country. In the west and north and a fair part of the south-east, the pattern of field and hedgerow, hamlet and farm that we know was already established. But over millions of acres between the Yorkshire and Dorset coasts, the country scene was still largely medieval. Perhaps 4,500,000 acres of arable land still lay unenclosed in the open-field system; and a much as a further seven million acres of 'waste' -open heathland and scrub - had still to be reclaimed. There were still more than a hundred thousand acres of wastes in Hampshire at the end of the 18th century, excluding the Downs, sixty thousand in Berkshire, and three hundred thousand in Devon.

It was from this period that the majority of today's aristocratic families date - comparatively few go back to before the Civil War - and it was in this period that the landscape of central England was constructed in the space of little more than two generations. It became so that the only respectable occupations for the sons of the gentry were landowner for the eldest, army officer or one of the professions for the second, and clergyman for the third. Their education was marked by the study of Latin, which permanently distinguished them from the sons of Dissenters, who were excluded from being Justices or holding political office, who did not quote Horace, and who devoted their energies to the building up of industry. In this way, status and snobbery dug themselves in to the countryside when they should have been broken. The House of Lords, temporarily abolished during the Commonwealth, was re-established; and while for the first time a capitalist society and a capitalist agriculture had been opened up, the gentry quickly muscled in on the latter to become the biggest capitalists of all. Their subsequent co-option of the princes of industry led to the preservation of paternalistic attitudes, and the belief in enlightened amateurism to which much of Britain's industrial decay has been attributed by authorities ranging from Lord Young, Secretary for Employment in the Thatcher government, to Labour party theorists.

This is the distinguishing feature between England and all her Continental neighbours: that the establishment of our aristocracy, our inherited system of land ownership, and our landscape, took place AFTER our Revolution. In mainland Europe, revolution and republican government resulted in land reform and the break-up of large landed estates. Here, the reverse was true. The end of revolution resulted in their consolidation.

The other vital difference is that inheritance in England has always been on the basis of primogeniture - eldest son takes all - whereas on the Continent, at least from the time of Napoleon on, the principle of division of inheritance was almost universally observed. In this way, both land reform and a large peasant class were preserved right into the present century. It often resulted in land's being broken into absurd and unworkably small holdings, but it did prevent the process of re-concentration of land into few hands. In England, the exact opposite held good: a structure of landowning and of society were reinforced which actually blocked these developments; and while large estates have repeatedly been broken up for economic reasons, the basic principle of freedom to acquire and control large areas of land has remained without restraint.

When Lord Derby instituted the New Domesday survey, the Return of Owners of Land, in 1873 in an attempt to silence agitation about the concentration of land ownership, to his embarrassment it revealed that 7,000 individuals owned 80 per cent of the United Kingdom; and that a mere 600 persons owned a fifth of the entire land. This situation is still surprisingly unchanged today. Eighty-four per cent of the land belongs to 6 per cent of the population; and 52 per cent of it is in the hands of one per cent. Over half of the food produced in this country comes from 10 per cent of its farms; 80 percent from 20.

It has had to wait until this century, with the expansion of the farming middle class, and with it the growth of owner-occupation, for significant change to take place: and when it came, it was change, not in fundamental attitudes towards landholding, but the war-induced explosion of agricultural technique. As we shall see, now that economic opportunity is contracting, the old dispensation is reasserting itself. In times of economic stringency, it is the middle class, the entrepreneur and the small family farm, which get squeezed.

We have come into the era of agricultural surpluses with a social system of land tenure which appears modern, but is actually imbued with the politics of the past. To return to Orwell, "the English ruling class has never developed into a bourgeoisie pure and simple. It has never become purely urban or frankly commercial ... So it comes that each new wave of parvenus, instead of simply replacing the existing ruling class, has adopted its habits, intermarried with it, and, after a generation or two, become indistinguishable from it." And indeed, although the liberation of the middle class, which had taken place during the revolution, laid the ground both for the Industrial Revolution and for our society to move forward into a phase of development for which the rest of Europe had to wait another century and a half, this is what happened. In the Industrial Revolution, as the new entrepreneurs acquired wealth from manufacturing industry, they quickly turned to acquire the status of the upper classes by using that wealth to buy country houses surrounded by estates; by founding minor Public schools to educate their sons in the manners of the upper classes, and then marrying them to the daughters of the impoverished aristocracy. Where they remained involved in industry, they acquired an autocratic, paternalistic attitude towards their employees which still today bedevils industrial relations and prevents fruitful communication between management and staff, or the development of the genuine technical competence needed by those who run industry.

The process started early, and is well-documented. Richard Arkwright, the inventor of the Spinning Jenny, bought land in Cromford, Derbyshire in 1776 and then sold it again in 1783 to finance the expansion of his mills. At this time, annual capital formation in the cotton industry was running at 5 to 7 per cent per year. In the early years of the 19th century, however, in the repercussions of the French Revolution and the crash of the 1790s with its associated building collapse which left Bristol's Georgian Clifton suburb half-built and crumbling for over two decades, investment faltered. Arkwright turned back to the dream of becoming a landed gentleman, and bought the Hampton Court estate in Herefordshire for a figure equal to 30 per cent of the total annual investment in the cotton industry, and 60 per cent of the yearly capital formation it enjoyed.

Other cotton maganates, the Peels and the Fieldens, the Marshalls in the flax industry, the big coal owners the Ridleys, the Cooksons and the Cuthberts, and Samuel Whitbread the brewer, all followed the same road. John Knight, the wealthy Worcestershire ironmaster spent £50,000 on buying a large block of Exmoor from the Crown at the phenomenal price of

£5 per acre, and spent years in an unsuccessful and financially disastrous attempt to farm it. And as their money moved into land, so they married into the aristocracy: the Foleys became baronets in the 18th century, the Wortleys became the Earls of Wharncliffe, Guest became Lord Wimborne, one of the Leighs married Lord Wilkinson's daughter. Only the Quakers, with their tradition of not marrying out of their own Society, failed to disperse their capital in this way. Already by 1793, both Robert Peel and Samuel Oldknow, major figures in the cotton industry, had become members ofthe Manchester Society of Agriculture; as had the steam engine builder James Watt. In this, the main flowering of the Industrial Revolution, technical breakthroughs demanded timely investment in extensions of plant: and already the purchase of land was tying up capital and retarding the extension of our industrial base.

It was industrialisation which enabled Britain to avoid mass starvation and maintain a relatively high standard of living. The Civil War and the Commonwealth had given us a social structure which encouraged enterprise, and the Enclosure movement and the growth of the cities had created a potential mass market, provided the capital and materials for the growth of industry. Relative political stability combined with a progressive agriculture and abundant market outlets and sources of supply overseas, and the great and growing commercial centre in London, to spawn the thriving textile industry on which industrialisation was built. But already the snobbish retreat back into the land was sowing the seeds of the industrial decay we are reaping today. It is interesting to note that the word 'snob' comes from the description 's.nob.' - sine nobilitate - after the names on the roll of university students of those not from aristocratic family - that is, those aping the manners and seeking the company of the upper class.

Now, on the land, the 20th-century middle-class farmer, whose land-owning dates only from the low values of the Depression, or from the post-war protection and support which allowed farming to generate enough capital to finance or repay land purchase, has again built himself into a social structure which is almost as rigid and change-resistant as that of feudal times. The difference is that the strength of that structure is now derived from economic forces rather than the strength of arm or sword. We have seen the develoment of a farming middle class which has rapidly moved to adopt the values, powers and self-justifications of the old landowners. And it is continually reinforced by a steady further flow of wealth generated outside farming. "Men who have made fortunes in industry ... are ready to invest their wealth in the purchse of agricultural land and buildings from motives other than those primarily inspired by a desire to engage in farming the land. Landownership in its own right has a fascination for them and acts as a magnet drawing wealth generated in industry into land," said D R Denman in his paper 'Land ownership and the attraction of capital into agriculture: a British overview' in Land Economics in 1965. The picture remains the same today, although more frenetically speculative. Young Stock Exchange executives, profiting from the 'Big Bang', are borrowing money abroad (taking out insurance against violently adverse movements in exchange rates), and using it to buy land to "set up the estates of the future. One of us had better know something about farming -" but the object of the exercise is investment in land value, not its productive use for society.

The excitement has been greatly amplified by the large movement of institutional money into farmland during the 1970s. At one time it was the fashion to be concerned about institutional buying of farmland. The inflow of money from insurance companies and pension funds into farmland has been publicly blamed for the sharp upthrust of land values in the 1970s which, among other things, encouraged a number of local authorities to sell off their smallholdings (thus removing one of the few remaining entries to farming for the young and those with little capital). So great was the concern that the government set up the Northfield Committee to report on this new and disturbing phenomenon. A reliable estimate of the total amount invested by the financial institutions in farmland in the five years up to 1983 was given at a seminar organised by the Centre for Agricultural Strategy at the Royal Society in that year. Mark Summers, Director of Hill Samuel Investment Management Ltd, said that it amounted to about 238 million. At £3,000 a acre, that represents about 16,000 acres per year, or less than one fifth of the annual turnover in farm land. There is little doubt that the major source of capital fuelling the land price rise has come from within, not from outside the industry.

A whole succession of tax measures has encouraged the process. The possibility, until around 1960, of using farming as a tax loser to offset against profits made from business, the still-valid exemption from Capital Gains Tax on a first home and its attached land, the 45% concessionary rate on agricultural land, the CGT roll-over provision (of which more later), income tax rebates on inputs to agricultural land on the same basis as investments in industry, the possibility of writing down farm improvements over a period as yearly running expenses and thus obtaining quicker tax relief on them, quite apart from the now much-criticised capital grants to assist increased farm output, have all increased the attraction of farmland as a home for capital.

Capital Gains Tax roll-over deserves particular mention: for it has worked as a powerful ratchet to consolidate existing farmers' hold on the land. The provision allows exemption from CGT on any windfall profits from the sale of land for development, whether for housing, industrial use or roadbuilding, if reinvested in farmland within two years. If the average figure is taken of 50,000 acres a year of farmland lost to development, this represents a very substantial sum seeking reinvestment.

In one Oxfordshire village, Stonesfield, in the course of 1985, two farmyards, each of approximately 3/4 acre, sold for little short of £200,000. A third is now on the market at a £quarter million. If this pattern is repeated, even just all over the south-east, the amount of money in farmers' hands chasing replacement farmland is more than enough to purchase all the agricultural land changing hands.

But what is most striking is the way that this wealth has immediately become attached to a whole social structure that has existed for centuries. In their classic analysis of the position of farmers within the power structure in East Anglia (Property, Paternalism and Power), Newby, Bell, Rose and Saunders showed how, in 1978, before the local government reorganisation, 42 per cent of rural district council and 29 per cent of county council members in Suffolk had agricultural interests, while the figure in Norfolk actually reached 50 per cent. Further, they were 'over-represented in gate-keeper positions within the councils.' Thirty-five per cent of farmer councillors held one or more council or committee chairmanships. Where they made up two-tenths of county council members, they still held three-tenths of chairmanships; and while three-tenths of rural council members ,were farmers, they held four-tenths of chairmanships. Moreover, 73 per cent of such farmer councillors employed labour, 42 per cent of them having more than five farm workers, at a time when only .32 per cent of farms in the area had other than family labour, and only 8 per cent had over five workers. Twelve per cent of the same individuals were JPs, 32 per cent lay churchmen, 26 per cent also served on water or drainage boards or other public bodies, and 87 per cent had other local responsibilities.

Once again, as with John Spencer in the 16th century, this paints a picture of public spirit and responsibility. "Moderation" and "independence" become synonyms for "don't rock the boat" and "blessed are those that have wealth, because everyone's better off for not disturbing them in their enjoyment of it." "Agriculture in Britain is still much more organised around the institutions of property than around those of occupation." says A Stinchcombe in his study of Agricultural Enterprise and Rural Class Relations. As E A Attwood comments, in another context, "The approach to agricultural affairs is a good indicator of the national economic philosohpy at any given time." It takes rigorous analysis to show just how far this also indicates that political power is still quite firmly in the hands of the large landowners.

Newby et al spell out how there was an opportunity for tighter planning control on farm buildings in the Vale of Dedham - the heart of the Constable country. Although planning controls normally only apply to buildings of over 5,000 square feet and more than 40 feet high, it might have been thought desirable on conservation grounds to bring in the Article 4 Direction requiring formal planning permission even for smaller developments in this sensitive area. In fact, a voluntary liaison system was preferred with arbitration as a backstop: so that farmers were simply asked to co-operate in informal discussions of their plans, with the final decision in any dispute being reached by a body in which Ministry of Agriculture, NFU and CLA representatives outnumbered planners. "We don't have many problems on planning matters," they quote an NFU official as saying: "we don't have sessions of getting together with all the district councillors who are farmers, or with county councillors. It's just an agreed attitude between us."

At the same time, planning committees, often chaired by farmers, resolutely opposed the development of any light industries in villages or country towns, thus incidentally keeping out any competing alternative employment in what is notoriously one of the lowest-wage areas of Britain.

Their account, on the basis of a widespread survey of farmer attitudes, of the systems of moral justification of this position of control, falls into three parts. Firstly comes what they terms the 'paternalistic', the "we know what's best for people" outlook. Next is the 'exclusive', which amounts mainly to preserving the beauties of the countryside for the landowners' own benefit and property values - which often expresses itself in a public concern for conservation. The last is the 'altruistic', which is summed up in the "stewardship" argument frequently used to portray the landowner as someone carrying the heavy responsibility of taking care of the national countryside heritage at little or no profit to himself. If conservation is left to the large landowner, it will be carried out "in the public interest", but not necessarily for the public.

The authors point out how these three weave together into a complex and robust fabric of authority imbued with respectability, in which farmworkers are involved by respect and acquaintance with an employer whom they know face-to-face, and thus recruited to accept and legitimate the continuation of privilege. By the same token, politics are personalised, with the candidates in elections being voted in on grounds of personal acquaintance and respect without declaration of any political position. It was noted that, only when urban and rural areas were combined into new districts under the local government reorganisation, did candidates begin to adopt party labels in their campaigning, Before that, 'keeping farming out of politics' had the happy effect of preventing the discussion of farming in open debate between the political parties.

In this way, the authors conclude, "Economically and politically-dominant groups are in a position to impose their values, beliefs and perceptions of the world onto subordinate and less powerful groups and thus to influence the latter's perception of the legitimacy of their situation. To the extent that this occurs, gross and manifest inequalities may come to be seen by all classes as natural if not desirable and established patterns of economic privilege, and political control may thus be perpetuated virtually without challenge. Clearly class relations are most stable when they are unquestioned: the successful manipulation of lower class perceptions and evaluations of their situation is therefore likely to be a highly significant factor in maintaining social and political stability."

This is of the essence of the English situation. Overt greed, gross exploitation or naked malignity do not exist - perish the thought! - but under an unshakeable assumption of the right to order things as they have always been ordered, acquisitiveness is actually satisfied - and justified because some of its fruits are spent on aesthetically approved ends. Exploitation does take place under guise of benevolent patronage, and the rural worker class - which includes the struggling small farmer - is held firmly in position at the base of the pyramid. As long as this situation continues, it will be impossible to address the real issues of conservation: which cannot be founded on an urban-based bureaucracy or handed down by a wealthy elite, but only on a broad participation by the whole of society. It needs to be both the soil and the fruits of the way people live and work, nurtured and sustained by a wealth of different economic activity. That this is possible is already demonstrated by the growth of conservation volunteers, the willingness of unemployed and those on MSC courses to become involved and committed, and the bubbling up of small rural enterprises which could, if given its head by planning administered with vision, transform the rural environment.

The new factor in the age-old picture is the advent of the

urban out-comers into rural communities. In the past decade, 4 per cent of the former urban population has moved out into the country, seeking peace and the cleanness of country life; and giving a sharp additional twist to the upward spiral of land values. This is why one house plot in a disused farmyard can now, in the south Midlands, fetch £18,000. If permission can be gained for a bungalow, the plot price goes to nearer £30,000.

In so far as its first interest is the protection of its own property values and of the rural dream that has led to the move from the towns and cities, this new element of the population finds itself naturally allied with the large landowner. "Conservation" rules, but it is the preservation of the view and of property values that count, not the conservation of the rural infrastructure or the fabric of the rural community. Thus the property-owning middle class joins the side of the traditional landowning ruling class under the 'exclusive' rationalisation. Also, incidentally, in opposition to the interests of the rural working population - the occupants of village council houses, those seeking other than farming or commuting employment. Until, that is, the landowner puts on his farming hat. In this, his businessman/paternalistic role, he may enlarge fields, use sprays and fertilisers, spread manure, burn straw and fall foul of the preconceptions of the newcomers. Here, he finds himself more naturally allied to the farm workers, who see his livelihood as their employment and security. This paradoxical two-way pull helps to maintain the inertia of the present situation.

Thus, by landowning, political and social criteria, the outcoming urban middle class, the middle-class farmer and the traditional landowner all find themselves on the same side of the fence for much of the time. Under conservation criteria, they will also be together as far as conservation protects and enhances property values. But where farm business criteria rule, the farmer and the new countrydwellers find themselves opposed. This is the new factor in the situation, and one which will increasingly disturb the traditional dispensation in the country. Oddly, it begins to be abetted by the forces of economics as we move into the era of general surplus of agricultural produce. Previously, the link between the farmer/landowner's enjoyment of his land and his business use of it as a productive resource was never questioned. When the market would not support farm production, the land was simply left unused. For the first time, the two are not necessarily identified: and a new force begins to wish to dictate the use made of the land. It is not surprising that this phenomenon should have shown itself earlier, and more strongly, in England than elsewhere in Europe. That is yet another aspect of the way that the development of our society is 'out of synch' with that of our neighbours.

In a very English sense, it is a revolutionary situation. In a very English way, the large landowner, whether aristocratic or high bourgeois, is likely to come through it largely unscathed, by appropriating the goodwill and respectability attaching to his status and his claim of altruistic stewardship. It is the small farm businessman who is most likely to have to face major, possibly shattering change. It is in the middle range - of economics and of social class - that the greatest probability of transformation exists. It is also the middle range of farmland - neither the top-grade arable nor the poorer or marginal upland - which is most vulnerable to change, as we shall see in the next chapter.

CHAPTER 4 THE GROUND RULES

Ye injur'd fields, ye once were gay,
When Nature's hand displayed
Long waving rows of willows grey
And clumps of hawthorn shade;
But now, alas! your hawthorn bowers
All desolate we see!
The spoiler's axe their shade devours,
And cuts down every tree.

George Crabbe (1754-1832)

The surface area of England, Wales and Scotland amounts to just under 23 million hectares - 94,249 square miles. Just over 5 per cent of this is virtually unmanaged - inland rock, lake, cliff or seashore. Another 5 per cent is covered by roads, railways, airfields and canals. Ten per cent is occupied by buildings, and a roughly equal area by woods. Fifteen per cent is moorland. The remaining more than half is under deliberate agricultural management

The island has a remarkably varied geology, containing almost all the known rock types. This variety is in turn worked upon by the climate -altitude, temperature, day-length, average rainfall (which varies from 200 inches a year in West Wales to as little as 25 inches in East Anglia as the clouds shed their Atlantic moisture on the journey north-eastward).

On that basis, man works his changes and modifications, and is in turn moulded and characterised. The parent rock in each area determines the form and material of traditional domestic building, the colour and nutrient composition of the soil and its workability. The rainfall regime, influenced by topography and its drainage effects, leaches, waterlogs or modifies the earth. This in turn indicates the natural vegetation and fauna, the most successful crops, and influences both the diet and the average health of the population which are somewhat conditioned by both the crops and the animal types traditionally grown, and by the mineral content of drinking water and foods.

Natural landscapes, the slow-changing woodland, and moorland with its strong, inherent rhythm, occupy little more than a quarter of the country. Two thirds of the rural landscape is visually affected every season by man's farming activity.

Of this two thirds, 65 per cent is, owing to soil, climate and topography, only really suitable for growing grass. It has no economic cropping use. The only way of converting the vegetation it is capable of supporting into agricultural production is through ruminant animals. To botanists, grassland is an "unstable ecological sub-climax". Without the constant, monthly discipline of grazing, it quickly grows out, becomes tussocky, dominated by woodier weed grasses and then by scrub bushes. Studies of lightly-grazed rough grassland over the time when the first myxomatosis outbreak decimated the rabbit population show clearly the progression from grassland to unlovely thicket to wilderness. Rush or thorns, weeds and wiry grasses will rapidly take over even quite good farmland; and the landscape become degraded.

The line between grassland and high-grade arable cannot be precisely drawn. Obviously, it will move according to the returns to be obtained from cropping. When, as under the Common Agricultural Policy, prices are maintained at an artificially high level, farmers will respond by cultivating land which would otherwise naturally lapse into pasture or be left unmanaged. As EEC agricultural prices are forced back down nearer to world market levels, the cost of continuing to cultivate land on the margin between grassland and arable will become prohibitive, and it will change use.

In the last major agricultural slump, of the 1930s, a great deal of heavy land, in what would now be called quality classes 3 and 4, fell out of use, being neither cropped nor even grazed. As a result, scrub took over, and the hedges met in the middle of the fields. Nor was it just in marginal or outlying regions that this happened: indeed farmers in those parts are accustomed to scraping a living in an almost cashless economy, making ends meet by maximising the use of family labour, and living off the land, so that their system is remarkably resilient. Where the changes were most striking was in the lowlands of central England.

It is in the borderline areas between land classes and farming types that the changes will show up most clearly as social and economic conditions vary. The extreme land types - steep, wet pastures of mid-Wales, the north-west and Devonshire, or the prime arable flatlands of East Anglia and Lincolnshire - are unlikely to change their use markedly, short of an economic or physical cataclysm. The line of instability runs between the grass two-thirds and the arable third of the country, roughly diagonally from the Humber to the Severn and Dorset. There are significant enclaves on either side - particularly the fertile lands of the Dee estuary on the 'non-arable' side, and the heavy clays of the Kentish Weald on the 'arable' - but as a broad picture the division holds good.

That this is fundamental, the product of geology, altitude and the higher rainfall as you approach the Atlantic, is beyond doubt. Poorer soils from less-hospitable rocks, wetter, less well-drained, steeper, less easily-manageable land, characterises the north and west of the island. The effect of this environment shows up in almost any map measuring historical and social development: whether it be the finds of Bronze Age beakers, tumuli, or successful modern arable farming. It is, in fact, another face of the "south-east tilt" which has become a commonplace in the mouths of sociologists and economists. Wealth, industry and property prices, general employment and farm prosperity all tend to concentrate in the south-east: and this is not just a phenomenon of the current recession. Britain's economic and industrial decline may have thrown it into higher relief; but, apart from the temporary upsurge of the Industrial Revolution which spawned potteries, ironworks, mines, wool and cotton mills in the less-favoured west and north, it has underlain the life of Britain since time immemorial. And, as European agriculture is forced to contract, that structural truth about the land will be underscored.

While the heavy lands of the Kentish Weald - like the Kent coalfields -may find alternative economic life flowing from the stimulus of being between the Channel Tunnel and London, and the Less Favoured Areas of the north and west will no doubt continue to be supported both by the EEC for socio-economic reasons and the British government for landscape ones, the whole fabric of the countryside could begin to wear thin in a great sash from Britannia's right shoulder to her left hip.

Speaking broadly, it is along this swath that the increase in cereal acreage has taken place over the past 10 years as EEC prices have drawn more and more farmers into this uniquely profitable activity. These same lands, during the Second World War, were ploughed up and laid down to wheat under the national campaign to increase home-produced food. They are, one might say, the agriculturally-arousable areas: those which most readily respond to changed economic incentives; and most clearly and massively display the landscape consequence of such change.

The flatlands of East Anglia have become dedicated to arable production over a much longer period. This is classic large-field countryside, where field amalgamations have been in progress since the 1950s. Livestock production in the eastern counties has declined steadily over the last 20 years, and is now at an irrevocably low level, both the buildings and the skilled workforce needed for their husbandry having been dismantled.

For this land, there is no turning back. Nor is it remotely conceivable that a quarter-century of advance in mechanisation and growing techniques will be relinquished. In national food-supply terms, this will remain the granary of Britain, the source of her major supply of vegetables, potatoes, sugar beet. As far as can be foreseen, it will continue to be economic to cultivate, and the methods and techniques of production, while they may be fine-tuned, will not be significantly modified. Nitrogen use may be made more precise as concern about nitrate levels in ground water increases; but in absolute terms, grade 1 arable land will be farmed with increasing intensity.

It will also maintain its value. While average land prices

across the country have, since the introduction of milk quotas and the realisation that production controls are definitely on the EEC agenda, diminished by about 22 per cent in real terms over about five years, large estates and holdings in the east have largely commanded higher prices than land elsewhere. This price steadiness expresses confidence about farming's future on that type of land. It also demands that production continues at the same, or an increased level, since a capital asset of such value, even if it is not supporting a high level of borrowing, will be required by its owners to show a commercial return.

In purely theoretical terms - or under a doctrinaire centrally-planned economy - it would be possible by the end of the century to produce all the home-grown food Britain needs from about ten counties. Agriclture could, at the turn of the century, be an activity that only takes place south-east of that line from the Humber to the Severn. East Anglia, and certain other areas uniquely suited to intensive, mechanised tillage using large machinery and crop varieties which respond well to synthetic inputs and produce well-standardised, easily-harvested and processed products, could become islands of intensive agriculture. The question is, islands surrounded by what? We shall return to that question in later chapters.

In fact, such an extreme situation is highly unlikely, The determination of the other EEC governments to support their small farmers, and the mounting public awareness of conservation and environmental issues, guarantee that agriculture will continue, albeit in an increasingly trammelled manner, in areas where a bald economic analysis would rule it out. Where landscape, wildlife habitat, ecological uniqueness, and urban recreation signify, farming will be supported provided it maintains the countryside to satisfy those ends.

It is anomalous, but quite English, that Britain's small farmers should be able to justify their existence on cultural and aesthetic grounds, while riding on the same vehicle as their more numerous and politically-significant European counterparts. The French government, although it has presided over a reduction of its agricultural population from ll to 8 per cent in the past 10 years, still has a very significant and vociferous rural vote to take into account. Indeed, a major plank of Jacques Chirac's recent successful election campaign was European preference and the need to exclude New Zealand butter and lamb.

In Germany, political stability in the early postwar years hung on small farmers, as was graphically depicted in the recent film Heimat, and the Iron Curtain was at one time effectively policed by them. Today, when the majority of small farmers, at least in southern Germany, are part-timers also holding industrial jobs for their main daytime income, the prosperity of the farming lobby is an esential pillar of society's idea of its own economic welfare; and farming activity serves as a sponge to soak up spare labour capacity in times of recession or early retirement. The degree of mechanisation and investment on holdings which in this country would not even be considered viable, must play a significant part in the total economy.

Interestingly, it was precisely these small farmers who were chiefly responsible for frustrating the early intentions of the Mansholt report, which laid down the objectives of rationalisation and regionalisation of agricultural production for the EEC. Those regions best suited to produce a given commodity, it said, should concentrate on it and serve the rest of the Community. On that basis, Great Britain, Ireland and Brittany, would have become the dominant areas for ruminant livestock; the Paris basin would have been the bread-basket of Europe; pigs would have been concentrated in Denmark, the Netherlands and Eastern England. North Germany might have specialised in dairying and sugar beet. What would not have happened, is a continuation of cereal production on small holdings in southern Germany remote from all the major centres of grain handling and shipping.

In fact, the German government fought a fierce rearguard action to obtain special subsidies to cover its grain producers' higher transport costs, and protect them from precisely the rationalisation pressures Mansholt intended to help improve the Common Market's efficiency and strength. Today it is still the German government which, all through 1985, resisted all moves to bring EEC cereal prices closer to reality.

As we have said, Britain has been historically out of synchronisation with the rest of the EEC. The process of rationalisation and farm amalgamation begun by the Enclosure movement, and kept on course by the system of primogeniture rather than division of inheritance, accelerated enormously after the war; and while other European governments are still treading warily at the pace of change, the fallout has already substantially occurred in Britain.

One consequence is that our farmers, as an occupational group, are no longer a significant electoral lobby. While, until the mid-70s they continued to command considerable influence for reasons of patriotism (their wartime record), sentimentality (as custodians of the much-idealised countryside) and simple respect for those who own land, once their postwar credit had been exhausted, environmentalists began to paint them in new colours of spoilers and exploiters of the land. Starting with Rachel Carson's 1960s classic, "The Silent Spring", a succession of books like Marion Shoard's "The Theft of the Countryside" and Body's "The Triumph and the Shame" built up a groundswell of opinion which made it gradually legitimate for urban envy to justify itself by pointing to rural greed.

It would not be fanciful to see in this the revenge of the displaced peasantry drawn and driven into the cities to provide the cannon fodder of the Industrial Revolution. Many towndwellers cherish a romantic notion of a countryside of which they have virtually no practical experience, but which they nonetheless feel is their patrimony. The old conflict between the landlord and the poacher has given way to the much graver incidents of the rustlers armed with crossbows. While respect may still be given to the owner of the stately home with its walled estate and its admission charge, it is difficult to see how the ordinary farmer can, in future, occupy other than a peripheral position in British society, since no future war is likely to be fought in terms of sea blockade which could give them a key role, acknowledged and appreciated by the rest of the population. Above all, because farmers are no longer the backbone of a thriving rural community, but have become merely isolated occupants of far larger areas of land than urban dwellers can ever hope to possess.

In the public mind, the average farmer is likely to be assigned a role midway between crafty bucolic fool and gardener. Where, in the Celtic and Cumbrian fringes, he can play these roles, he will be supported by the same means as his more robustly self-interested Continental cousins, but without the respect still felt for peasants in nations less long separated by urbanisation from their rural roots.

On prime land, farmers may continue to be able to run successful large businesses. They will not need support, and will be able to command both respect and compensation from the public purse for any concessions they make to environmental concerns.

But in the middle, between these two extremes, will travail a large number - as many, for instance, as the coal miners - who have a less important role than formerly: farmers in middle-grade land who have responded to the economic indicators given them by successive governments and the EEC by moving into cereals, and who, as the cereal business leaves them behind, find that the door back into milk production has been slammed by quotas, and that beef production, already unrewarding, is being squeezed too.

Moreover, living in parts of the country not cherished for their grandeur or picturesqueness, they will not have the park-keeper role open to them either. Finding a viable way of life will, for them, demand a great deal of research and experiment, and a large amount of analysis. These have as yet hardly begun: and no other significant crop has yet presented itself as an alternative which could absorb a million hectares and bring an economic return.

CHAPTER 5 THE URBAN OCTOPUS

If to the city sped, what waits him there?
To see profusion that he must not share:
To see ten thousand baneful arts combined
To pamper luxury and thin mankind;
To see each joy the sons of pleasure know,
Extorted from his fellow-creature's woe.

Oliver Goldsmith: The Deserted Village

By the year 2000, nearly half of the world's population will be living in cities. The trend towards urbanisation is massive, inexorable and world-wide. By that time, London will have dropped off the bottom of the list of the world's twenty largest conurbations: the only developed country cities still amongst them will be Tokyo, New York with North-eastern New Jersey, and Los Angeles. The rest will all be in the Third World, ranging from Mexico City through Sao Paulo, Calcutta, Bombay, down to Buenos Aires, Istanbul, Jakarta and Manila.

What this implies in terms of human history and society is still a matter of guesswork. It can be argued that human beings as a species are natural village-dwellers: that like many other animals they need to live in a group which is small enough for them to recognise and be recognised by the majority of their fellows; and that when placed in conditions of mass numbers and anonymity, mental ill-health, crime, instability of relationships, family breakdown and mutual aggression all increase. When moved even into the most squalid urban living conditions, they tend to set about creating urban quasi-villages which satisy this basic need for a network of supportive threads of acquaintance and mutual reference.

Modern urban development, particularly with the advent of

buildings of a more-than-human scale, and without provision of controlled spaces and regular locations for social encounter, is demanding completely new ways of living and relating. It is a depth and abruptness of change for which evolution has had no time to equip us, and is producing grave effects in the process.

The European countries were uniquely privileged in this matter. At the time when our populations were booming, we simply sailed off round the world and quite ruthlessly seized large tracts of other peoples' countries in which to settle. It does not need much reflection to see our reaction when the new developing countries, whose populations are in turn soaring, look to us for space to settle their more enterprising and adventurous members. It can be seen in action every day at every immigration point in this country.

But it is salutary to read, for instance, the Sri Lankan theologist Tissa Balasuriya, in his book Planetary Theology, spell out just how far European Christianity has served over the centuries as "an ideological superstructure for the domination of one group by another" - as far as race, class and sex are concerned: but it takes a true sense of humour to savour his delicate irony in suggesting that, perhaps, all the New Zealanders should move to live in Australia so that New Zealand might be re-settled by Bangladeshis; and the Canadians decamp down into the western states of the USA to leave Canada vacant for some of China's surplus population.

Having built our economies on a position of command in both banking and commodity trading; having reached a mature stage of industrialisation and a domination of the world trading system which guarantees us wealth and privilege and has allowed our populations to stabilise, we are able to sit back and behold the recreation of Dickens' London a hundred times over and a thousand times larger in Brazil, Mexico, Indonesia, India, Iran, Iraq, the Phillipines. We should not, however, have the hypocrisy to imagine that this is due to their poorer management of their affairs. They, like us two centuries ago, are facing the same inexorable forces, but scaled up by the world economy of the multinationals, the politics of the superpowers and the supersalesmen of the arms trade. The differences of organisation are due to accidents of timing and fragments of good fortune.

The Scandinavian countries, blessed with small populations for their surface area, which have in the past two generations made a relatively smooth transition from a land-owning rural peasantry to a property-owning urban bourgeoisie, still with strong ties to the land, can well afford the luxury of a good environment. Still in touch with their folk roots, most Finns will own a countryman's wood-carving knife, and use it on weekends in their lakeside cabin. Finnish glass designers, when short of an idea, will step outside and look at icicles; textile designers use the clear primary colours and rustic weaves of their countryside. So do the Swedes, who were so shocked when their Prime Minister was assassinated, and presumably never paused to think that, after all, he could, in many other countries, have been gunned down by ambitious army officers, or hanged by a political rival after a show trial, all with the connivance and encouragement of international corporations who saw their commercial interests threatened by his social democratic creed - had Sweden not already arrived safely at an powerfully self-sustaining equilibrium of land and capital distribution.

Again, the fact that the French and the Dutch are so much better than the British at co-operation is not due to their inherent superiority or a difference of social attitude and values. The French co-ops are able to handle nearly half of France's mighty cereal marketing and export trade, and the Dutch ones to act as equals to the multinationals on the world commodity market when buying raw materials for animal feeds, because, when the Depression was at its deepest, they were two populations of peasant landholders, all of roughly similar size and powerlessness, who thus felt a sense of solidarity and perceived the need to collaborate in order to stabilise their markets and protect their interests as a class.

In Britain at the same time, with a free market in land and a tradition of relatively large independent farm holdings, we moved instead in the direction of individualism and "independence". Many of today's major farming figures owe their start to being able to buy land at rock bottom prices during the slump. The Rex Pattersons of this world, and indeed many Scots who took land in the 1930s in Lincolnshire and East Anglia, saw that they could make money from land provided they could buy it cheaply enough: and proceeded to set themselves up as capitalist farmers and soon enough as gurus and technical authorities too.

Now we have come full circle. With land prices beginning to drift downwards again, and weakness in the economy stark and evident for all to see, the less fortunate of farm entrepreneurs are finding the boards move under their feet. The difference, this time round, is the growing popular demand from the urban population for the return of what they feel to be their birthright - even if was taken from them generations ago. That demand is, increasingly, expressed in terms of challenge and confrontation. The prospering industrial worker, now a home owner, feels that owning bricks and mortar places him on a footing of equality with the landowner, and asks who is he to refuse the right to walk, camp, and traverse his land. It's our country, and it's a free country, is the cry.

Nor is it merely the new property-owning class which feels this resentment at the farmer's possession of his fields. The recent invasion of a farm in Somerset by a hippie convoy, while arousing outrage and leading some people to offer to form armed vigilante bands - a prospect which the farmer rightly declined as being far worse than the evil he already had to contend with - expresses a fundamental demand: a feeling of entitlement to use, enjoy, and benefit directly from the fruits of the land. It does not matter that the use in question is ignorant, ill-organised, or destructive in effect. What is important is the basic, irrational conviction of entitlement. The same feeling has been expressed by the squatters movement in the 1970s, when buildings bought for demolition and then left empty for months or years by property developers were taken over and occupied in order to return them to productive use. 145 Park Lane was perhaps the most glaring example of conspicuous speculative waste opposed by immediate housing need. A similar example was provided by groups of landless farmers who occupied estates in Chile and Portugal.

In developing countries, as Joe Foweraker has shown in his Latin American study "The Struggle For Land", the availability of land makes a profound difference in the development of society and the economy. The fact that free land was available at the frontier in the USA during the 19th century meant that there was always the alternative of "Go West, young man" for the enterprising worker, so that he could escape the 'double mill' of landed property and the capital power of industry in the cities. In Russia, by contrast, serfdom tied the peasant to the land, to be sold as a possession with it. This prevented the Russian serfs - apart from those who fled - from open frontier land taking, or indeed from migrating into the cities. It was serfdom which was primarily responsible for delaying Russia's industrialisation.

In England, no such immobilisation of labour took place. The rationalisation of land holding, the driving out of the poor to prevent their becoming a charge on the parish, their migration into the towns and cities - where, firstly, there was some chance of employment, secondly freedom from the comprehensive control by the landowner/JP, and thirdly, as a last resort, more chance of making a living by crime and escaping apprehension and punishment - prepared the labour force for the industrial concerns started by the Dissenters when the Restoration excluded them from political or public office. It was easier to snatch a bag and disappear into an urban warren, than poach a rabbit and be hanged for it; easier too and more rewarding to become a toiling mine or factory worker than be driven from parish to parish in the country, branded as a vagabond. It is the descendants of this land-deprived class who today are returning to stake their claim, by tourism or by force, to the countryside.

Once again, this is a function of population pressure combined with dispossession. To return to Scandinavia, which has suffered from neither to any severe degree: in Finland the people enjoy an ancient, common-law 'Everyman's Right', whereby anyone may enter any forest, whether privately or publicly-owned, camp, fish, pick any mushroom or berry. The income derived from selling berries, fungi or wild fruits is officially free from tax. Indeed, the equivalent of the Spar grocery chain acts as a collecting network to which people can bring their pickings for onward transmission to the canning, preserve and drink industry.

The fruits of nature are recognised by the Finnish

government as an important part of the country's economic resources. Although there is a special 3 to 4p bonus per litre paid for milk produced in the northern areas near the Arctic Circle, with only a 130-day growing season for fodder, many poorer farmers actually need to supplement family income by sending their children out commercially picking wild berries.

In the profusion of the brief, heady summer, it is possible to harvest a litre of bilberries or arctic cloudberries in five minutes; and the latter, which make a particularly-prized liqueur, as well as a sauce served with some meats, can fetch up to 35 Fmk per litre in a good year - nearly £5. The 10,000 residents of the northern parish of Suomussalmi, for instance, in 1983 earned 300million Finnmarks by their berry- and mushroom-picking activities - about £3,800 per head (the national average income being then around £5,250). It is a casebook example of individual-scale rural enterprise being encouraged, and contributing both to economic and social stability; and to an attitude which values natural resources.

There are special one-week courses run by the National Forestry School to train 'mushroom advisers' in picking those varieties that are useful in the kitchen and, above all, those for which there is a good commercial market; in turn, the advisers will pass on their knowledge to their own parish. The Finns eat far more kinds of fungi than we do. False morels, cooked three times to remove the poisonous factor, are highly prized; and they also know how to prepare and enjoy milk caps - normally regarded as inedible by other European races. Chanterelles command a particularly good price from the processors. In England, we are so far detached from this kind of folk knowledge that we can only buy such things in tins, expensive restaurants or speciality shops.

The insistence on everyone's right of access to the forest is not because large areas are state-owned. In fact it is only in some of the roughly one-fifth of the forest areas which belong to the government -mainly in the north - that the public is excluded from certain parts which have been declared nature reserves. The vast bulk of Finland's forest -nearly three-quarters - is in private hands; and the major part of that is held in lots averaging 46 hectares (110 acres) by small farmers, to whom it is an important source of income.

This in no way prevents their allowing their compatriots freedom of access - and being confident the right will not be abused. If a camper wants to light an open fire, he must ask permission of the owner of the land. Otherwise it is asumed that his concern for the environment will be as great as that of the person whose name is on the title deed. Landowner and visitor share the same social status, experience, values and concerns.

This little digression serves to illustrate a number of the points which are central to any consideration of conservation and countryside access. To speak of these things as if they were simply a matter of social or cultural maturity and responsibility, without taking into account the relative shortage of supply of countryside in proportion to population, and the long historical deprivation of a large part of the urban population of the pleasures of the land, is foolish arrogance. Nor is it surprising if a whole class which has been systematically so deprived - for the economic benefit of the land-owning and entrepreneurial class - is ignorant, crude and inexperienced in its enjoyment and use of these things when it finally gets its hands on them. The Return of the Wild expresses itself as much in the urban dweller who drives out into the country to dump his black plastic bag of garbage in a ditch, or the hordes of ramblers who are rapidly eroding the Pennine Way, Ben Nevis and Great Gable, as in a special piece of new broadleaf planting. All three are enjoyments of free space; and the difference between them is a matter of values, experience and understanding.

And here we come onto the nub of the matter. As Cotgrove has pithily remarked, one man's Utopia is another man's dystopia. A great deal of the conservation argument is not about genuine conservation at all, but preservation, which is a very different, and sterile thing. It is about the preservation of a privilege enjoyed by a relatively small section of the population. Genuine conservation is a living and life-enhancing process to which many of the urban disenfrachised, - unemployed, MSC groups and volunteers - contribute: and often strongly resisted by elements of the preservationists. Preservation, says Cotgrove, "consciously or not, is elitist. A tiny minority of self-appointed arbiters of taste dictates what the living standard of the rest shall be... It includes the ancient Establishment, the landed aristocracy, Oxbridge, the officer class and their hangers-on, and trendy academics with less pretensions to gentility who prove their clubworthiness by espousing these elitist views." In an iconoclastic study in Built Environment, David Eversley estimates that, allowing for overlaps, the total membership of all the architectural 'conservationist' bodies does not exceed 10,000 - one hundredth of one per cent of the population. "They do not always agree among themselves, but have one common denominator, and that the lowest: that no change is better than change, that their taste is better than that of any architect or planner in public service, let alone in the service of a private entrepreneur. They are certainly mourning for a past when they and they alone had the right to tranquillity, the open countryside, distant coasts, spacious surroundings, plentiful and humble servants, and were in receipt of the safety and convenience provided by public expenditure. They loathe the extension of these privileges to the majority of the people... And they have contrived to divert public funds on a large scale away from demolition and rebuilding towards the freezing of the status quo."   Building conservation (stately homes apart - to which, some members complain, the National Trust is devoting an ever-greater part of its resources, in neglect of its original purpose of safeguarding the most valuable landscapes) is a mainly urban concern. But the same strictures may be applied to a significant part of rural conservation. Preserving open land untouched is frequently given a higher value than a by-pass which could allow a village community to live and breathe again; and keeping building in expensive traditional materials to maintain the "tone" of the neighbourhood preferred over flexible modern housing that could meet the needs of a younger population (as well as making a worthy 20th-century contribution to the fabric of the countryside). More truly than can be said, this brings us back to the hold on land and power established by the landed gentry at the Restoration, and never truly relinquished since: a world of "medieval communal securities rooted in church, family and guilds - traditional forms of order and hierarchy - and, it must be said, essentially illiberal."

The same values were forcibly exported with the Empire. As Professor Ali Masrui has pointed out in his book "The Africans", one of the things that the colonials went in search of, even more consciously than wealth and economic power, was space, beauty, peace and an escape from the encroaching squalor and development of a growing industrial society. This they truly found, together with a very equable climate, in the uplands of Kenya. Today one can still walk into the Kericho Tea Hotel and find the easy chairs, the smell of Gold Flake cigarettes, and the lovely prospect of gardens with flame trees and ornamental shrubs, the grand piano, of many a grandparental drawing-room. The question is, whether this is a world which has a right to exist today,or whether it can continue to do so without intolerable deprivation for those upon whose backs it rests. For just down the road there is likely to be the solitary African wife, working a smallholding barely large enough to feed her and her children, whose husband has migrated to Nairobi to live eleven months of the year in a shanty town and seek £30-a-month employment which may give him enough to return to his family for the twelfth month, but little to bring them. This monopolisation and sterilisation of the countryside by wealth and power is also to be seen, in less extreme forms, in this country - but none the less real for that.

It involves a much wider section of our society. Eversley says, in towns, "small old shops stock specialities for the wealthy minority; supermarkets lower the cost of living for millions." But in country towns and rural areas, the reverse is true. Small village shops cater for those who cannot afford private transport: and when the supermarket chains move in, they actually behave in classic colonial fashion. First they out-compete all the local food retailers and put them out of business; then all that they contribute to the local economy is an often small part of their initial construction costs plus some relatively menial employment. Normally, management is brought in from outside; and such raw materials as are locally purchased are sold back to the local community, and all profits then taken out of it to a national headquarters. (If a supermarket were locally-owned and community-based, it would then contribute the best of both worlds: central buying power and central shopping, combined with a broad range of employment without disenfranchising the local population. But that is not the normal case today, when four large national supermarket chains control 43 per cent of all food retailing in the country.)

Once again, we are back to the advancing demands of urbanisation. The question is not, whether a traditional countryside is a good and beautiful thing to be preserved at all costs, but whether within the constraints of satisfying the reasonable needs of a population of 56 million, it can, or should be. This in turn depends on agreeing a definition of reasonable needs, and above all, who imposes or enforces that entitlement. In considering this, it may become evident that many of the Utopian prescriptions for preservation and proper management of the countryside are based on a very narrow and quite unrealistic assessment of the situation. For instance, the age of mass flying has demanded the expansion of airports, taking in large tracts of farmland; and the workers' holidays spoil the private beaches of the affluent around the Mediterranean. It would be a very daring autocrat who would offer to turn back the clock on either development - and he would have not to own any shares in an airline or a package tour company.

In fact, some of the largest landowners look upon popularly-demanded conservation as impertinent interference in their rights: or virtually as Communism, and the biggest farmers are likely to be well tied, in intensive farming methods, as junior partners, to the very supermarkets which behave as classic primitive colonists in the countryside.

Thus again, the powers of land and capital combine to work against genuine conservation and real life for the rural areas. And the short-term economic interests of the urban disenfranchised are yoked in an unholy alliance to their interests. Nowhere is this seen as clearly as in the drive towards home ownership, which has acted as the perfect shilling to recruit ordinary people into the army which supports the big economic interests: the large national spec builders, the land owners and speculators, and the big farmers whom Roland Machin, a partner in the estate agents Savills, urged in August 1986 to "tap the demand for development land as an alternative crop." He did not mention that you can only get one crop of houses on a given piece of land; and that this process is the cement which seals the tomb of a living countryside.

The urban dweller who buys a building plot on the edge of a Cotswold village and puts up a pleasant five-bedroom house for himself, is likely to be in the forefront of resistance to any development of light industry in the village which could provide a range of employment for the indigenous population; and will probably also oppose the building of smaller homes for rent or sale to families of lower socio-economic status, lest it reflect adversely on the value of his property. The villagers are all right, so long as they stay in the council houses at the other end of the village and go into town to work. If they grew up in, and inherit, cottages but cannot afford to stay in the village, these can be bought and gentrified, and appreciate nicely in value in the process. In 1985, when the government was boasting of an inflation rate of less than 4 per cent, rural property values in Oxfordshire, within easy commuting distance of London, have increased by 15 per cent, which represents a massive inflation in the cost of housing, one of the major components of the cost of living for the ordinary employed person.

In the economically buoyant south-east, the first step onto the ladder of ownership of land, bricks and mortar is the great divide between the haves and the have-nots; and is clearly perceived to be so by an increasing proportion of the population. Young blue-collar tradesmen and their fiancees will scrabble to get a mortgage on a spec-built ticky-tacky box on an estate, even if it means both working overtime and postponing having children. Young marriages are often observed to collapse under the strain.

Richard Body, in his book Agriculture, the Triumph and the Shame, makes much of his calculation that up to £3.35 billion per year may have been sucked into agriculture during the 1970s and capitalised in land values: thereby depriving manufacturing industry of that amount of capital which could have been used to renew or improve its competitiveness. In fact, a significant portion of the money invested in agricultural improvement and development is immediately re-cycled into local enterprise and services -drainage, building and fencing - and a good bit more - in the way of machinery, agrochemicals and food processing - into the national economy. But the building societies lent out a greater sum, 3.873 billion, IN ONE MONTH, June 1986, to house-buyers chasing the upward spiral of property values. And thus, despite our boast of having reduced inflation figures to the fingers of one hand, we witness the cost of the most basic human need, housing and shelter, soar out of the reach of anyone on the national average wage or less.

The actual cost of building a decent 4-person, two bedroom house today is around £25,000. But the cost of a site to put it on is, in central southern England, a further £18,000 - or over 35 per cent of the final market price of £51,000. This inflated charge, which arises directly from speculative gains attached to control of land, is what puts housing beyond the means of the young family, the vigorous young worker, on whom the future of the country and the life of the economy actually depends. The natural pride of a new couple making a home, and the energy and output they would naturally invest in it, is being frustrated purely so that those who have cornered supplies of land - without which no construction, industry or production is possible - may make unearned profits. Nor is it simply the owners of land who profit from the system. Mortgage tax relief enables the lenders of mortgages to charge higher interest rates than would otherwise be feasible. Similarly, the subsidy is partly transmitted through higher house prices to housebuilders' profits, land-owners' revenues and the wealth of sellers of second-hand houses. A whole system has been erected on the back of inflating property values.

Moreover, whereas in previous property booms, profits made by "trading up" have been used to reduce borrowings, in the one of the early 1980s, there has actually been a steep increase in total borrowing: in other words, (actually, those of the Bank of England) for the first time, "there has been a major withdrawal of equity". Increasingly, it is being used to finance current consumption: in fact, mortgage advances taken on the back of inflating house values, have become one of the major engines of our economy. A gamblers' economy, not one of genuine work and wealth creation. Obviously, it is cheaper to borrow at the net-of-tax mortgage interest rate than from a hire purchase company. And a great deal of the demand thus created is satisfied, not by our own industry, but by mounting imports.

The contrast with the situation on the Continent is striking. In Germany and France, households generally do not move once they have bought a house. While trading-up is important in Britain - and indeed fuels the upward price spiral as new profits from sale chase new-built assets - in France and Germany it is virtually unknown. Further, the control of housebuilding in this country by a few very large volume speculative housebuilders who are able to outbid any other prospective buyer of land, whose whole operation is increasingly geared more to emphasise land development gains than organise production, who rely increasingly on subcontractors rather than maintaining a trained workforce of their own, has rendered the private sector increasingly incapable of satisfying housing need, either in terms of quantity or quality.

Finally, the sale of council houses, as well as creating a new class of homeowners who are statistically the most likely to get into difficulties with mortgage payments if the economic recession sharpens or unemployment spreads further, has taken up nearly 10 per cent of the building societies' turnover. This is a major source of the 'high demand for mortgages' which has prevented a significant reduction in interest rates for all other house purchasers. Council house sales have actually further excited the whole paper chase, boosted profits for the financial institutions and removed the need to offer either lower interest rates or better deals for minority groups. All in all, a greater sum is currently being locked up in the property cycle each month than is invested in manufacturing industrial capacity per year: a sick and topsy-turvy economic situation.

The diversion of such quantities of resources into non-productive investment is nothing short of a national tragedy. We have become a nation of property speculators. And, it may be clearly demonstrated, the entire process, as well as being morally and economically debilitating, once again reinforces the trend toward privilege for one section of the population over another. In the nine years from 1976 to 1985, the proportion of mortgages granted to first time buyers has declined by 12 per cent from 53% to 41%. One major house-builder, Barratts, has cut the number of house starts aimed at first time buyers from 70 to 31 percent of its output. Despite the fact that the 1960s birth rate bulge is now into adulthood, the young are no longer a viable market for homes. Building societies actively prefer to lend to people with a good track record - that is, those who are 'trading up' in the course of following the speculative spiral.

The countryside implications of the rapid expansion of home ownership are twofold. The first is the rapid growth of housing estates around market towns selected as growth points by the county authorities and the rising pressure from building groups for relaxation of planning restraints on development in Green belt and rural areas. One consortium has recently put in a strong plea for four new "village communities" to be built in the counties of Essex, Sussex and Surrey. For "village communities" read "suburban outmovers seeking quality of life and property values enhanced by a rural setting."

The second is what I shall call conservation wobble. For the upwardly mobile homeowner, as I have said, conservation means conservation of property values: of the peace, cleanliness and the view he has bought. Traffic, or the development of homes for others, will tend to be viewed with suspicion or resentment. But so will the traffic, activity and any pollution created by the farmer whose work has over the centuries created the environment into which the homebuyer has now chosen to move. It is actually a dead hand, arresting and strangling the life of the countryside and embalming it in a financial mausoleum: opposed to both the community and economic life and constant change on which the countryside depends.

So while he may share the farmer's liking for a handsome house with a well-planted garden, and the absence of industry (which could push up wages for the few workers the farmer employs), he will resent the farmer's burning of his straw for crop sanitation reasons, or the smell from his piggery. And so, from an agricultural point of view, he becomes associated with the intrusive rambler, the litter lout and the vandal. This should not hide from us the truth: that any genuine system to preserve the life, the richness and the vigour of the British countryside will have to be people-centred: based on reinvigorated communities of people who actually work where they live, and bring up and educate their children in those communities. It will require in some ways a great deal more flexibility in planning, to allow clean, flexible industry into villages, to encourage the work from home which the modern information communication revolution has for the first time made possible, and a great increase in commercial and productive activity. It will have, however, to exclude the use of the country simply as a dormitory by urban commuters, or an investment either by non-participants in the rural community or the farmer to whom the land is simply a factory floor (and the larger the better). For he and the urban outcomer behind his cypress hedge and his high gate represent the same force for economic stagnation.

It is an urbane, velvet-gloved version of the Brazilian landlord who hires gunmen to terrorise peasant squatters off land that he wants to press into use to rear beef as a cash crop for his own profit rather than allow it to feed the country's own population.

CHAPTER 6 POLICY OPTIONS - THE REAL STORY

In 1985, the Nature Conservancy commissioned a study of changes in land use expected by the years 1990 and 2000, and their implications for conservation. In a rather simplistic exercise, the consultants projected most crop yields forward at current rates of yearly increase, took the resulting accumulated surplus of output over demand, and divided it by average yield per hectare. This gave them a projection of 910,000 to 1,250,000 ha (2,184,000 to 3,000,000 acres) of land not needed for production by 1990, and 2,380,000 to 2,860,000 by the year 2000.

The prospect of nearly 3million acres having to be taken out of production in the next 13 years is a shocking one, with immense implications for both the landscape and the rural economy and population. Fortunately, such a drastic move is not likely in such literal terms. It does, however, give a strong indication of the kind of pressures farming and the countryside are likely to be subjected to before children born today have even left school.

In a far more sophisticated study carried out by the Centre for Agricultural Strategy at Reading University, a set of four possible Common Market scenarios were projected using the Newcastle University macro-economic model, the Land Classification system developed by the Institute of Terrestrial Ecology and a new 'Reading' model developed especially for the purpose.

As a marker from which to measure the other possibilities, the first scenario was a 'Current Trends' one, positing that current trends in prices, incomes, output levels, agricultural structure, factor returns and so on were allowed to continue unregulated. While support prices would drift gently downwards in real terms, the steady increase in yields (running at about 2 to 3 per cent per year) would lead surpluses and their budgetary cost steadily to increase, the study showed. In particular, total cereal production was shown as reaching equilibrium at 22 per cent above the 1984 level (then a historical record) of 22.5 million tonnes, with wheat in particular, increasing by more than 31 per cent.

A second option, labelled the 'Free Trade' one, assumed a complete adoption of Free Trade with large parts of Europe's food requirements being bought on the world market - the course beloved of critics such as Body. Hill livestock headage payments and support for agriculture in Less Favoured Areas would be abolished, and the production, consumption and profitability of UK agriculture would be determined by the free market. The unexpected result of such a move - quite the reverse of Richard Body's dream of a reversion to the livestock production 'natural' to this country - was that wheat production would actually increase, since the relative fall in wheat prices was much less dramatic than that for other products. Obviously, if world wheat prices fell further, this effect would be less marked: however the boost to demand arising from Europe's increased imports is more likely to push them up. In any case it exposed the pitfalls of making simplistic assumptions about economics.

Another, almost equally surprising conclusion the study produced was that, while lowland livestock production was highly susceptible to pressure on returns, upland sheep farming is remarkably robust. On reflection, this is logical, since hill sheep farming is much closer to a subsistence economy - with all that implies in terms of resilience - and far less dependent on expensive bought-in inputs. Whether the numbers of shepherds would keep up, is another question, the researchers pointed out. Even here, there is room for management to become more extensive, and less labour-intensive. The conclusion is, in any case, a far cry from the conventional assumption that poor hill and upland is the most truly marginal.

Implicit in this scenario is a massive blow to the farming sector, resulting in a sharp devaluation of farm assets, particularly land, as well as a reduction in the level of intensity. "Clearly, in making this adjustment, many farmers would be bankrupted, but their assets would be taken over, at substantially lower prices, by new farmers and by those wealthy enough to survive the financial storm, and land would generally be expected to remain in agriculture, albeit at a substantially lower level of production than currently, although those areas with alternative and remunerative uses would probably leave pure agricultural production. These are likely to include field margins, wet patches in areas of good quality land, as well as land in those regions more usually identified as 'marginal'."

The political realities and the violent uncertainty of such a course make it even less likely to be pursued. A third scenario, titled the 'Prices' was thought more probable, . This envisaged a 15 per cent co-responsibility levy being imposed on cereal production, and one of 5 per cent on beef, with milk quotas being held at their 1985 level, so that all three of the major food mountains were being squeezed. The likelihood of a levy of this size's actually being imposed in the near future was also thought small: the proposal for a 3 per cent cereal levy having been vigorously resisted in the 1985/6 farm price settlement. However, international pressure against Community protection from our competitors -particularly the United States - will continue to mount; and the study points out that the least they would be likely to accept is a levy large enough to cover the costs of surplus disposal (such as is already imposed, for instance, by the Finnish government on its farmers). This works out at 15 per cent, which is a fair indication of the real level of price support enjoyed by European farmers, as opposed to the levies on current imports, which are very much higher.

This course does have the effect of cutting cereal production, by just over 10 per cent. But since it does not reduce the sale price of cereals, it brings no benefits in the form of cheaper feed costs to livestock producers, and thus does relatively little to alter the horn vs corn balance in any radical way; indeed the study shows a concomitant further reduction of 6 per cent in livestock output. A steady and purposeful cut in cereal prices paid to producers would adjust the balance more - and thus automatically precipitate surplus and budgetary problems in other sectors, particularly the grain-fed livestock sectors such as pigmeat and poultry; but is likely to be even more strenuously resisted. Co-responsibility levies are likely to be regarded as more acceptable in extremis by those EEC member governments most resistant to attack on the cereal sector, if only because they are susceptible to exceptions - for instance for small farmers. It is significant that, whereas 84 per cent of all German farms grow some cereals, and 57 per cent of these cite cereals as their main occupation, only 3.5 per cent have more than 30 hectares. Indeed, the United Kingdom is the only EEC member with significantly more than 10 per cent of holdings over that size; whereas in all of France, Denmark, Ireland and the Benelux countries more than 75 per cent of farms growing cereals do so as their main occupation. In Denmark, these comprise 92 per cent of all farms; and in France, 66 per cent. The NFU's complaint of "discrimination" in the face of co-responsibility levies from which small farms are exempted, is indeed the cry of the larger landed interest.

The painful slowness of adjustment in the CAP probably means that, in the end, just as occurred in the dairy sector when the EEC subsidy had reached the level of £125 per cow, crisis measures may well have to be taken in the form of production quotas. In this 'Quotas' scenario, where all production is limited to the level required for the EEC to be self-sufficient, the study projected a 15 per cent drop in cereal production, with wheat output being axed by a dramatic 39 per cent. If farm quotas are able freely to be traded, this would wipe out the product mountains at a stroke: but since it would not involve any cut in the sale price of cereals, it would still involve the same 6 per cent reduction in beef and veal output as well, and an overall drop of 2 per cent in total livestock output. It would also further strengthen the position of the larger versus the smaller farmer. In fact, although just as this book goes to press, something like the 'Crisis' scenario has been adopted for the milk and beef sectors, cereals - which are a vastly larger and more entrenched problem, remain at present untouched, except by a gentle down pressure on price.

As we have seen in Chapter 1, the land most vulnerable to

change of use is actually the lower grades of lowland, which are in danger of falling between the twin stools of cereal and livestock production. And while this might come out of cereal farming, there is little indication that it would switch to the more mixed type of farming often associated in the public mind with a more desirable rural environment.

A fifth scenario was considered in the study, but proved impossible to model with existing information and computer programmes. This was the 'Green' option, which would take the 'Quotas' scenario as its starting point, and use the substantial amount of EEC money it would save (some £545 million, the study suggests) to give grants encouraging conservationist farming systems. The problem which immediately arises is how these are to be applied and administered. In the first place, there is little agreement as to what constitute desirable components of the countryside. Many different people want different things. Secondly, there are no clear parameters linking CAP components to environmental changes. Past research has been so single-minded about increasing food output that we do not now know how to stimulate farmers into workable conservation channels. The whole thing is at present in the realms of theory and personal opinion. It is in any case highly unlikely that a single national policy would be right for all areas. Nature does not always agree that the law should apply equally to all.

At present, a start has been made, with the offer of substantial payments to support lower-input farming in six selected Environmentally Sensitive Areas. Elsewhere, the Wildlife and Countryside Act has made a tentative start with management agreements, under which farmers are paid to use less-than-economically-optimal methods on certain areas of land in order to maintain their ecological character. But if this practice were to be extended generally, it conjures up a frighteningly large bureaucracy exercising control over huge areas of the country. Visions of the War Ag Committees established during the last war to monitor and, as necessary, control production levels and practices, are not too far from the truth: an agriculture ruled by Big Brother - or Big Sister. It may be that this is what some conservationists would like; but it must be recognised that a countryside regulated by prescription - a system of 'heritage sites' surrounded and possibly linked by 'conservation zones', all in a sea of 'agricultural and forestry landscape', as proposed in a recent study, "Countryside Conflicts" - is very different from the landscape we grew up with, know and love. That, quite clearly, just growed, like Topsy, and was the product of a complex interaction of social, economic, agricultural and local market forces. Forces that may now have been overtaken by other, more powerful technical, political and economic ones, but which cannot be replaced by diktat.

In the most comprehensive examination to date of the history of rural settlements, "Village and Farmstead", Christopher Taylor has shown that the pattern of the English countryside has been a living, labile thing, constantly in flux, flowing as population mounted in times of prosperity, such as in the Mesolithic era, in 5000 BC, where there is clear evidence of a systematic attack on the primeval forests, and consequent soil erosion; under the Roman empire; and in the 16th century as human numbers recovered from the disaster of the Black Death. It also ebbed during times of famine and pestilence or economic hardship. All that seems to have been fixed since time immemorial is a series of territories, occupied in turn by extended families, tribes, estates: within these, villages and farmsteads were set up, drifted as the soil became sour or debris accumulated, died out in times of weakness, or when a powerful landowner wished to re-plan his estate. It was not until the 16th and 17th centuries, as population climbed back up to 4 to 5 million for the first time since Roman times, that the positions of villages became relatively fixed. Although the names of many modern villages are found in Domesday, these are attached to areas rather than specific settlements. It is only as population and wealth rise to the level where there are strong competing demands on the land that change ceases to be free-flowing, and the system starts to shudder and grind. Even in the first half of our own century, during the great Depression, there has been a massive reconstruction of land tenure, as many of the old landlords were forced to sell, and a new class of farmers established themselves with a lower fixed cost structure. It may be that we are starting to see the same process over again.

times, that **the positions** of villages became relatively fixed. Although the names of many modern villages are found in Domesday, these are attached to areas rather than specific settlements. It is only as population and wealth rise to the level where there are strong competing demands on the land that change ceases to be free-flowing, and the system starts to shudder and grind. Even in the first half of our own century, during the great Depression, there has been a massive reconstruction of land tenure, as many of the old landlords were forced to sell, and a new class of farmers established themselves with a lower fixed cost structure. It may be that we are starting to see the same process over again.☎ Already, the gathering pressure on the farm economy is having its effect: in the past two years there has been a clear and increasing downward drift in agricultural land prices. From a peak of £4,935/ha in June 1984, by April 1985 the average price of land sold had come down by 23.5 per cent. Estate agents reported that a great deal more land was available for sale than was being offered - for fear of pushing the market down - and lenders acknowledged that some of their customers were being forced to improve liquidity by selling off small parcels of land. In the one month of July 1986, the average price of farmland sold dropped by a further £1,000 per hectare.

This is still some way from the kind of crash in land prices that took place in Denmark in 1981, where bank lending to farmers had been allowed to rise in the expectation of a never-ending inflation in land values, and many farmers - particularly young ones relatively recently entered into business - suddenly found themselves under-secured, while high interest rates were in many cases eating up three-quarters of their revenue, and progressively eroding their equity. However, it has to be said that, despite trimming its sails in response to milk quotas, the British farming community is, at the time of writing, some £6 billion in debt to the banks.

Clearly, this is not evenly spread over the whole body of farmers. Many are still farming inherited land, or land bought cheaply before or just after the war, and their businesses have a very advantageous fixed cost structure. Others have managed to acquire land and expand their holdings to a very viable size by using windfall profits from sales of land for development. But a significant number will have borrowed heavily to invest in land and equipment during the boom years of the 1970s: and it is on these that that £6 billion debt is bearing most heavily.

Allowing that between 1 and 2 per cent of farm land changes hands each year, it is likely that up to 10 per cent of farmers wil have built themselves into this high cost/heavy borrowing structure during the decade of the 1970s. If the squeeze is applied sharply, this suggests that numbers of farm bankruptcies or forced sales in 1987 could be rising into the hundreds, and on the way to four figures. In 1984 the number was only 35 nationally: by 1988 it could be in the thousands.

Already, as I write, an extraordinary case is going through the courts, of a Welsh farmer who is sueing his bank for lending him too much money, alleging that it pushed him to buy land and invest in expanding his dairy herd to twice the size he thought viable, just before milk quotas were imposed. In all parts of the country, small parcels of land being sold off to improve liquidity are a common sight, and a symptom of a still-concealed situation.

It has to be remembered that the financial structure of farming is not strictly rational from an accountant's point of view. The Newcastle University computer model has an 'optimum' structure, in which Gross Margin is maximised nationally, and the present level of production is achieved with the greatest efficiency. In this, there are already roughly a million hectares (9.5 per cent of the land in current use) labelled as "Low Gross Margin land", which, on a strict cost efficiency analysis, would be released from production. Making this adjustment would only improve the gross national product from farming by 1.7 per cent: however, it illustrates the basic immobility of farmers as a profession. As C W Spedding, professor of agriculture at Reading, told the RURAL conference in 1985, "Farmers aren't profit maximisers: they are fuss-and-bother minimisers." This means that very great resources of family capital, non-farm income, and belt-tightening, will be drawn on before major change takes place in the structure of farming. Nonetheless, the economic vice that is tightening is a huge and inexorable one: and change there will be. And it is here that the situation in Britain is quite distinctly different from that, for instance, in France.

While we are a small, densely-populated country with many competing pressures on land and a limited supply to satisfy them, France has roughly twice the area for a marginally smaller population. It is the major agricultural country in Europe. The French have realised, said an editorial in the Country Landowner in May 1986, "that the doctrine of comparative advantage favours France - cereals in the Paris basin, milk in Normandy, wine in Bordeaux and Burgundy, fruit and vegetables in Provence. Underlying all the protectionism that any French political party is bound to advocate is the knowledge that in a truly European market the best French producers would do very well indeed. This explains the equanimity with which the French view huge stretches of their country going out of food production. A figure of six million hectares (15 million acres') of France ceasing to serve any agricultural purpose in the next few years provokes only a shrug of the shoulders."

In Britain, we cannot afford such insouciance. Strictly speaking, there is no surplus of land in this country: only a surplus of labour and capital. We cannot afford to pursue a strict accountancy approach to agriculture, because 10 per cent of all employment in this country is now agriculture-dependent, and because the spiritual and recreational needs of a large urban population, as well as the basic need for a healthy environment, also have to be satisfied. In that sense, it can be argued that the build up of large-scale intensive farming producing surpluses of crops for export on the world market, is "perverse development", in much the same way as the creation of huge plantations growing cash crops for the profit of a land-owning elite in Third World countries has often acted against the fundamental needs of their peasant population, taking the best land away from subsistence farmers and forcing them to migrate into the towns and cities. The difference is that the poverty of our peasantry and our urban working class is not acute to the point of starvation, as is theirs. The industrialisation of our society has generated a great deal of wealth which is now available, despite relative economic decline, for the support of the land-deprived section of the population.

Ironically, it is that sector, or a part of it, which will exert increasing pressure on the countryside - compounding the economic pressures generated by agricultural surpluses - and which has the economic, and increasingly, political, resources to make that pressure effective.

This is where the present capital structure of farming, and the national love-affair with landowning, become highly significant. Historically, we have gone through the stage known to economists as 'primitive accumulation', where a small group of owners assemble economically viable holdings of land and launch into capitalistic farming. We have also, on all but a few of the great estates, emerged from the era of 'authoritarian capitalism' where, as still in many developing countries, those whose holdings were too small to be viable have been forced to give up their land and sell their labour to the land-owners as a workforce held captive either by debt or social structure. We have arrived at a mainly middle-class farming structure (albeit still with many of the social trappings and attitudes of a benevolent aristocracy) whose typical business size, form and financial structure is unique. Unlike other industries, it has not moved on to develop new structures, except as a means to maintain individual ownership of land. Only ll.8 per cent of all British farmers have more than £20,000 of tenant's capital (stock, equipment and self-financed buildings). Only 7.7 per cent have more than 500 acres. Barely a third have more than £20,000 worth of total assets, and only 31.2 per cent have more than £20,000 networth after liabilities. The average farmer, whose holding may have a theoretical value of half a million pounds, after selling up and clearing his bank overdraft, is likely to walk down the road with about the same as the average mortgage-paying home owner.

As the University of Reading Miscellaneous Study No 62 says, "In this industry of relatively small businesses, joint stock finance of farming is still virtually unknown. It is as if a century of development in business forms in other sectors of the economy has left agriculture unaffected." In other words, land ownership has taken precedence over either social or business development. Where expansion and intensification have taken place, it has normally been on the basis of private ownership. The smaller farmer's attachment to his own holding has been co-opted into the machinery reinforcing the hold of capital on land - whether the capital of the large landowner, the supermarket chain with its massive buying power, or the multinational company. In all cases, these are forces fundamentally urban in character. The larger landowner will generally tend to connive at the advance of urban interests for his own profit, even while preserving his own environmental privileges. And the urban small- and medium-fry investor will reinforce the trend with little or no understanding concern for the countryside itself.

The current economic situation faced by farming is not unlike that of the Great Depression of the 1930s. The difference is that there is a great deal more cash, wealth and optimism available in the rest of the economy, a fair amount of which, for both traditional and modern reasons, is looking for rural living space. Not only do a third of all farmers have additional incomes - 20 per cent of them their major incomes - drawn from outside farming: an increasing number of non-farming town dwellers are seeking to take up country residence, often adopting some farming activity part-time. While in 1960 only 4.9 of Home Counties farmers were part-timers, by 1975, in a ring with a radius of 60 miles from London, that proportion, had risen to 36.6 per cent. In non urban-influenced areas, only a third of farmers are part-time, while near London, a tenth of all holdings of 25 acres or less are farmed part-time. What is more, the level of investment increases steeply as the city is approached. Within 20 miles of London, a 1975 survey found average tenant's capital per acre stood at £86. Thirty miles out, it dropped to £56/acre; and at a distance of 40 miles, it was only £47.

This pattern is reproduced all over the parts of the country which are within striking distance of towns, or which have an established tourist, recreation or amenity use. The Farmers' Weekly of May 15 1986, headlined its Land section "Big Demand for Small Farms". It went on to list an extraordinary range of sales: stretching from a holding near Ivybridge in Devon, just off the end of the M5, which had in the previous week fetched £4,615 an acre, largely because it also had a "dilapidated 12th century farmhouse", through a 38-acre stock farm in Herefordshire that had realised £2,630/acre, and a 101 acre dairy farm near Torrington Creamery with a 358,000 litre quota, which fetched only £1,800/acre, to a 98-acre grass farm near Carlisle which was withdrawn from auction when bidding failed to reach the reserve.

In a world where the move to urban living is accelerating at a dizzy pace, England's uniquely rich natural environment is apparently subject to the reverse trend. The pressure of townees moving out into the country in·search of what they conceive to be the wild, could combine with the economics of a technically over-successful agriculture to bring about irreversible - but in truth fundamentally suburbanising - change in some areas of the countryside. Their economic clout will make those changes virtually irresistible, and render them profound also in social and environmental terms. At the 1986 Nottingham Town Planning Conference, a spokesman for CoSIRA, the Council for Small Industries in Rural Areas, forecast that 10 per cent of city dwellers - another 5 million people - will move out into rural areas and small towns in the next three decades. It is a collossal demographic change, and creative thinking needs urgently to be done about the basis on which they are to be accommodated.

Again, some parts of this movement will less viable than others. In the 1930s, when planning legislation was far more permissive than today, large areas of the Langdon Hills in Essex were sold off in plots of 1 to 5 acres to Londoners wanting homes inthe country to retire to: who then put up jerry-built wooden bungalows on smallholdings on which they never succeeded in growing anything because the heavy, three-horse clay land was too hard to work. It created a classic rural slum, which the would-be pioneers' heirs subsequently sold off.

A recent CAS conference on Alternatives for UK Agriculture heard that the farm enterprises most capable of expansion to soak up some of the spare acreage, were sheep, goats and horses. (It is a truism to mention that producing a given food energy value through a livestock enterprise requires ten times the space as the same quantity from arable.) But here again, the urban amateur element creeps in, with generally deleterious effects on the landscape. Already, there are at least half as many horses in this country as there were in the days when the horse was the sole source of motive power on the farm: they now occupy 15 per cent of all lowland grassland. Forty per cent of them are kept in the counties around London, and the growth of suburban horsiculture is making a significant, and generally ugly, mark on the land. While the keeper of animals for production - milk, wool or meat -will be aware of the need to look after his pasture as the most basic of his productive resources, to the pleasure-pony keeper, the paddock is only a parking lot, and the animal's lax grazing habit rapidly allows it to deteriorate into an unkempt, weedy mess embellished only by jumps improvised from oil drums and painted poles.

But while some attempts at "country life" will come and go, the general trend will be towards irreversible urbanisation. Land once acquired will be held on to because of its capital cost, in a steady transition from private paddock or non-viable hobby smallholding, to realisation of its development value and infill building.

In a significant part of the remainder of the countryside, a great deal of ingenuity and some radical thinking will be called for to prevent change of a very different kind: change often more accurately described as decay. The next two chapters will examine and attempt to evaluate two of the main prescriptions for averting that decay.

CHAPTER 7 ORGANICS: AN IDEA WITH A LONG WAY TO GO

The fresh harrow-lines seemed to stretch like the channellings in a piece of new corduroy, lending a meanly utilitarian air to the expansive, taking away its gradations, and depriving it of all history beyond that of recent months, though to every clod and stone there really attach associations enough and to spare - echoes of songs from ancient harvest days, of spoken words, and of sturdy deeds.

Thomas Hardy: Jude the Obscure

One of the favourite ideas for solving the agricultural surplus problem, restoring health and beauty to the countryside and finding a good use for land which modern farm technology would otherwise make redundant, is a return to natural or organic farming methods. In some quarters, this is also linked with vegetarianism, which is variously recommended because is less extravagant of resources, more moral, or does not involve cruelty to animals. It is important to examine these various positions and separate those which are practical and beneficial, from those which are idyllic imaginings or quite simply not feasible at all.

Beginning at the extreme end of the spectrum, it has to be said that the Vegan case - which shuns the use of any animal products - is extremely unsuitable to the climate, geology and life of this country, and if implemented on a large scale would bring appalling consequences in its wake. There is no place in a Vegan world for farm animals at all and, while the fact is seldom advertised, its creation would have to be founded on a slaughter policy of Hitlerite dimensions. All that might survive would be a few wild pigs in low-grade forests - which could not be allowed into any commercial tree plantations for fear of damage to young seedlings, and would still have to be illegally hunted to prevent their overrunning the country. Also, perhaps, a Hindu situation where diseased cattle were allowed freely to trample the crops and scavenge in dustbins because no one was allowed to prevent them.

Further, anything up to half of the British countryside would have to be abandoned to revert to unlovely and unproductive scrub and wilderness. While an individual's right to forswear all animal products for religious or philosophical reasons must be respected, the position is clearly untenable as a prescription for the country at large. And that is because it ignores one simple fact: that the numbers of all populations must be managed: those of farm animals as much as those of mankind. In the absence of such management, they will ultimately be limited by famine, pestilence or predators; which may fit into an apocalyptic vision of the world, but are hardly to be recommended as a day-to-day system of world organisation.

Vegetarianism which embraces at least the use of dairy products and animal fibres for clothing is rather more workable. But it still ignores the fact that, in the world at large, vegetarian diets are most natural in areas which have climates suitable for year-round arable crop production but less suitable for intensive grazing; or where competition between human and animal populations for land use is more intense, either because of the fundamentally low productivity of the soil or because of population growth and poverty. It cannot be often enough said that animal production is both natural to these islands, and can well be afforded in them, even without imported inputs. Indeed, precisely because the production of food of the same calorific value through animals takes 10 times the space it does from crops, animal husbandry offers the best - perhaps the only real - way of extending land use to take up the space no longer required for surplus cereal production, as well as maintaining the landscape we value.

And, indeed, this is well recognised by all realistic and experienced organic farmers. True organic farming is effectively impossible without animals: because their manure and bedding is a vital component of the soil nutrient cycle. Without it, soil fertility and water-retaining capacity can scarcely be built up: the logistics of a manual or mechanical harvesting of plant material for compost making on the scale needed in an agriculture without animals are frightening - and would depend on a huge expenditure of fossil energy. The great virtue of animals is that they do carry out this harvest for us with comparatively little organising; collecting useful nutrients in a form that we cannot directly digest, often in places we would find difficult of access.

In a fascinating essay in his book "About Looking", John Berger describes the change that has taken place in the last two centuries and a half in man's relationship with animals. It parallels the change in our relationship with, and perception of, the countryside. Berger shows how, in all primitive and ancient societies, animals served both as a reminder of the uncertainty and fragility of our own life, and as a support to it. As food, as draught power, as opponent to pit our wits against in the hunt, and as metaphor for our own emotions and powers.

Today, as draught animals have been completely banished by the internal combustion engine, and the spread of suburbia has created an environment where wild and domesticated animals are comparatively rarely seen, animals have become marginalised. As man has become increasingly trapped in isolated small family units, living in a consumer competition with each other which has also destroyed the ancient interdependence of human communities, animals have been either turned into artificial, unreal parts of the family, or reduced to a spectacle.

In popular culture, from Beatrix Potter to Disney, animals are only considered insofar as they can be made the vehicles of human problems, habits and attitudes of mind. Pets - a wide-scale phenomenon unique to the present age - are likewise deprived of their old, natural functions as guard dogs, hunting dogs, mice-killing cats: sexually sterilised, limited in exercise, fed on artificial foods, deprived of almost all other animal contact, their existence only justified by their completely dependence upon their human owners. Mere appendages.

At the same time, the zoo and the wildlife park go hand in hand with a constant spate of books, films and television programmes which allow us to become voyeurs of an animal world quite beyond our reach, and of which we have almost no real understanding. Wildlife photos which depend on cameras which can see in the dark making exposures faster than the human eye is capable of, to freeze and encapsulate the unseeable: these complete the packaging and removal from reality of the animal kingdom, indeed of all Nature. It began with the Romantic Revolution which idealised the Gothick and the awesome; it ran in parallel with the Industrial Revolution which made the majority of mankind into alienated urban dwellers; it is witnessing "the marginalisation and disposal of the only class who, throughout history, has remained familiar with animals and maintained the wisdom which accompanies that familiarity: the middle and small peasant."

It expresses itself today in the urban out-mover who takes a house in the country, seeking a dim memory from Grandfather's time of a country that is no more, or pursuing a quite synthetic fantasy ... and objects to the smell of the farmyard or the piggery, or opposes the establishment of a small business which could give employment to redundant farmworkers or their wives.

It is not extreme to point out that the concept of the countryside as a place of beauty is the province of a relatively small section of the -mainly urban - middle class. The true countryman or woman still has a practical, down-to-earth knowledge of it in all its demands and exigencies; the urban working class wants little of it, and knows less. Children evacuated from the cities to the country during the last war were amazed to find that milk came from somewhere else than bottles. An urban worker's use for the countryside is likely to be practical and quite close to that of his rural counterpart: fishing, coursing and the like. Some of the young urban unemployed may, through MSC or conservation volunteer programmes, become acquainted with the needs of the real natural life of the countryside. But the great public concern for "the countryside" is virtually the monopoly of those who were read Joyce Lankester Brisley's stories of "Milly Molly Mandy who lived in a nice white cottage with a thatched roof" in their childhoods. And of the large landowner to whom it is of value because it is the source both of his wealth and his political and social power.

And because the urban middle class is the culturally dominant one in the nation, it also has the ear of the media, which give its concerns, fears and prejudices disproportionate currency: to the point where a far larger portion of the population, which does not even know that a cow must be brought to calve every year if her supply of milk is not to dry up, is now convinced that the countryside environment is being destroyed by modern farming methods - a proposition which can be seriously called in question simply by going up in a balloon and looking down at it, in most parts of the country.

But I digress. My argument is that vegetarianism and Country Lifeism are both more products of the current spiritual, social and economic state of development of British society, than practical or even helpful prescriptions for the land. Without a genuine community involvement - and a genuine benefit to the quality of life of the whole community, conservation will remain confused with preservation, and vapid rather than vigorous.

None of which is to deny that the more mechanistic aspects of large-scale arable farming have tended to simplify landscape in areas suitable for their adoption, to reduce the range and variety of flora and fauna; even, to weaken the structure of some of the more fragile soils. However, if an argument is to carry weight, it must be measured, not wild or exaggerated. In the only large-scale comparative trial of full 'insurance' spraying versus a lower level of agrochemical inputs using them only when weed infestation or disease reached set danger thresholds, the East Anglian Experimental Husbandry Farm at Boxworth, near Cambridge, has confirmed that modern cereal fungicides do decimate some classes of natural insect predator. But such is the range of potential predators (some 30 or more) that the rate of removal of the harmful aphids which carry the barley yellow dwarf virus disease, was not measurably reduced. Moreover, it was found that the natural wildlife populations could only be prevented from migrating back quite rapidly once the spraying season was past from neighbouring small woods and hedgerows, by creating exclusion zones surrounded with an impassable plastic wall both above and below ground. Nature is more resilient than we give her credit for.

Elsewhere, the Gamebirds Project, has found that, simply by refraining from spraying a six-yard strip around the edge of a cornfield and accepting a 25 per cent yield drop from that area, insect populations remained high enough to support the full former size of grey partridge chick families which had previously been depleted by the lack of their natural food and the weedy, open cereal habitat they thrive in. It is much more likely that the adoption of this kind of measured neglect of field margins and corners will bring about the elimination of a good part of cereal surpluses, than the total abandonment of whole fields. A side benefit is that it is with precisely this field border area, richer in wildlife and natural wildflowers, that the passing walker comes in contact.

Indeed, this kind of finer tuning operation appears far more likely to achieve real progress in making farmland use more benign than the more outlandish suggestions of set-aside or husbandry revolution. Current concern about nitrates in ground water is completely ignorant of the fact that these come mainly from the soil's bank of mineralised nitrogen, not newly-applied fertiliser. Modern crop varieties have been selected to take up fertiliser N with very great efficiency, three times that of those grown in the old days of rotation, and missing only a tiny fraction of that applied. It is soil disturbance - and, particularly, the bare soil of fallows - which frees it to wash downwards. What is now percolating down to underground watercourses is likely to have been unlocked when long-standing permanent pastures were ploughed up during the last war. Setting land aside without a crop to cycle the soil nitrogen will not stop it coming out, as has been proved on land at Rothamstead which has received no dressings this century.

The comments of W J Jordan, proprietor of the Crunchy breakfast food company, are indicative: "We at Jordans got together some years ago to discuss the possibility of getting most of our cereal requirements grown without chemical residues. Whilst we had been buying crops grown organically for some years, we had to discount that standard due to the fact that it did not seem likely that we would be able to source 10,000 tonnes and upwards in the foreseeable future. Also, the high premium required for that grade was not going to allow us to compete competitively with other manufacturers in the supermarket arena."

Jordans' small throughput of 10,000 tonnes represents less than half of one per cent of the British cereal crop. To satisfy even that need, they have had to set up the Guild of Conservation Food Producers who contract only to use types of fertiliser which do not aggravate soil acidity, only 'soft' fungicides (that is, those which have been established not to harm insect populations), and no actual pesticides at all. Selective herbicides, too, are permitted. Finally, the growing of Conservation Grade cereals is all done under contract, with a guaranteed premium for conforming to the standards, procedures and materials laid down. This has pioneered a standard of farming "which seems to fit our requirements in as much as 'it was credible to the customer, realistic for the farmer and allowed us to aspire to higher standards later."

This move has been strongly decried by the Soil Association, the central body dedicated to promoting and policing true organic farming, as threatening to degrade standards. In an ideal world, that may be so. However, despite a Soil Association survey carried out in 1986 in the Newbury and Reading area, which found that a cross-class majority of shoppers were prepared to pay a premium for organically-grown produce, the facts of the present and immediate future supply suggest such a world is still remote. At present, despite the fact that retail demand for organic produce has been estimated at anything up to £34million a year, there are only a handful of growers to the approved standard. And while their numbers have gone from 200 in December 1985 to 300 in mid-1986 and may reach 400 by the end of 1987, they are mostly concentrated in Wales and the south-west. For any grower to become one of their number, he or she has to go through a two-year conversion process (certification will not be given without a sufficient time for chemical residues in the soil to have been broken down), suffering a yield drop without any premium to compensate meanwhile. Further investment in machinery for mechanical weeding, plus an increase in labour,

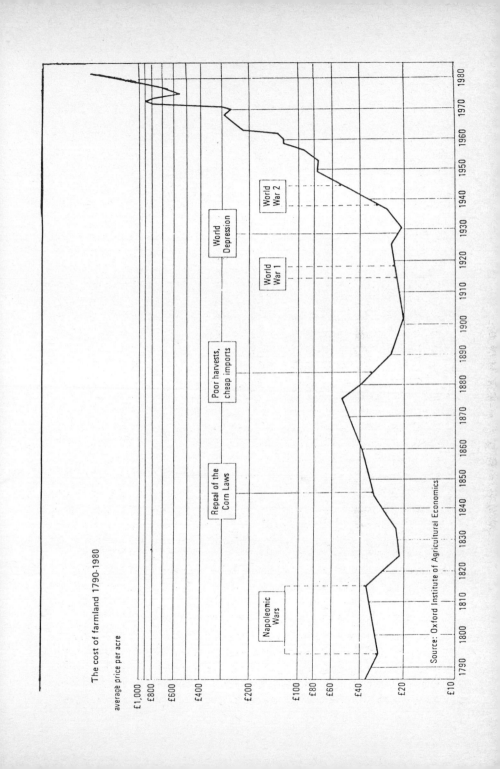

The cost of farmland 1790-1980

average price per acre

Napoleonic Wars

Repeal of the Corn Laws

Poor harvests, cheap imports

World Depression

World War 1

World War 2

Source: Oxford Institute of Agricultural Economics

£1,000
£800
£600
£400
£200
£100
£80
£60
£40
£20
£10

1790 1800 1810 1820 1830 1840 1850 1860 1870 1880 1890 1900 1910 1920 1930 1940 1950 1960 1970 1980

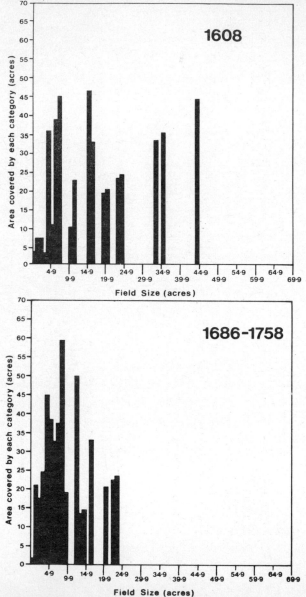

Fig. 5
Historical Changes in Field Size
(taken from maps of five estates in Worlingworth from 1608–1979)

The effect of the Enclosure Acts in the 17c and 18c is obvious

Source: Melinda Appleby, Suffolk County Council Farm Conservation Officer.

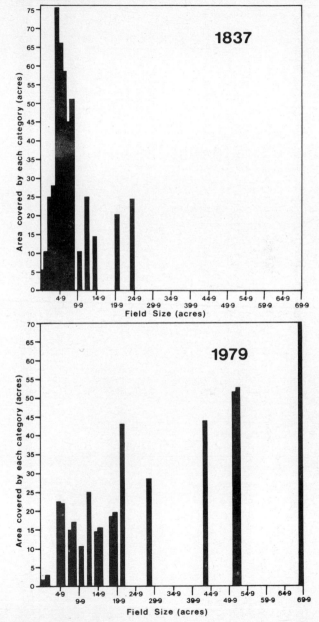

Table 2.

Urban Population (Millions)

	1970	1975	1980	1985	1990	1995	2000	2010	2025
World total	1,361	1,561	1,776	2,013	2,286	2,599	2,952	3,761	5,107
More developed regions[a]	695	753	802	849	897	944	992	1,080	1,192
Less developed regions[b]	666	809	974	1,164	1,389	1,654	1,959	2,681	3,915
Africa	82	105	137	177	229	293	370	570	958
Americas	330	374	422	475	533	592	653	778	960
Latin America	163	198	237	280	326	373	421	518	662
Northern America	167	176	186	196	207	219	232	260	298
Asia	494	589	688	798	928	1,084	1,267	1,697	2,400
East Asia	259	298	331	362	398	445	503	644	869
South Asia	236	291	358	436	529	639	764	1,053	1,531
Europe	304	326	344	361	376	391	405	427	453
Oceania	14	15	16	18	19	21	22	26	31
USSR	137	152	168	185	202	218	234	264	306

Source: *Estimates and Projections of Urban, Rural and City Populations, 1950-2025: the 1982 Assessment* United Nations, New York, 1985
(a) Northern America, Japan, Europe, Australia, New Zealand and the USSR.
(b) All others.

Table 3.

Distribution of Urban Population (Per cent). Size class of city

	Under one million					One million—Four million					Four million or more				
	1970	1980	1990	2000	2025	1970	1980	1990	2000	2025	1970	1980	1990	2000	2025
World total	68.2	66.0	62.8	59.2	56.8	18.0	18.2	19.5	20.9	18.6	13.7	15.8	17.7	19.9	24.6
More developed regions[a]	67.5	66.6	66.7	66.0	67.4	18.3	19.3	19.3	20.7	19.8	14.2	14.1	14.0	13.4	12.8
Less developed regions[b]	69.0	65.4	60.3	55.8	53.6	17.8	17.3	19.6	21.0	18.3	13.2	17.3	20.2	23.2	28.2
Africa	81.1	72.6	63.8	55.5	50.5	12.3	22.1	27.3	24.6	15.6	6.6	5.3	9.0	19.8	33.9
Americas	58.8	57.4	54.4	52.2	53.1	20.4	21.8	21.9	23.8	20.3	20.8	20.8	23.6	24.0	26.6
Latin America	64.7	60.9	54.8	51.6	52.7	15.0	17.3	17.9	20.3	17.6	20.3	21.9	27.3	28.1	29.7
Northern America	53.1	53.0	53.9	53.3	53.9	25.6	27.6	28.3	30.2	26.5	21.2	19.4	17.8	16.5	19.6
Asia	67.5	65.4	61.9	58.0	55.8	17.9	15.1	17.2	19.2	19.0	14.6	19.5	21.1	22.7	25.1
East Asia	62.8	63.0	62.8	62.2	60.9	16.2	16.8	16.8	18.7	19.8	21.1	20.1	20.4	19.1	19.4
South Asia	72.8	67.6	61.1	55.3	53.0	19.8	13.5	17.2	19.6	18.6	7.4	18.9	21.6	25.1	28.4
Europe	68.9	69.9	70.0	70.2	72.5	19.9	18.7	17.0	17.7	16.6	11.1	11.4	13.0	12.1	10.0
Oceania	63.3	48.9	44.2	41.0	43.1	36.7	51.1	55.8	40.3	41.3	0.0	0.0	0.0	18.8	15.5
USSR	84.7	77.9	76.6	73.6	74.1	10.2	14.4	16.2	19.5	20.0	5.2	7.7	7.3	6.9	5.9

Source: *Estimates and Projections of Urban, Rural and City Populations, 1950-2025: the 1982 Assessment* United Nations, New York, 1985
(a) Northern America, Japan, Europe, Australia, New Zealand and the USSR.
(b) All others.

Abandoned Bronze Age farms on Dartmoor. Aerial plot reproduced by courtesy of the Royal Commission on Historic Monuments.

Land available for energy timber growth; total suitable, and total after constraints (e.g. Nature Reserves, areas with water problems, and more economic alternative agricultural uses). Study by Institute of Terrestrial Ecology, Energy Technology Support Unit et al.

100,000 hectares	total suitable	after constraints
Highlands and Islands	468.3	264.2
Grampian	90.5	45.5
Tayside	102.5	53.9
Strathclyde	194.7	79.2
Central Fife	59.5	27.4
Borders, Dumfries & Galloway	130.0	63.2
North England	168.8	76.2
North West	82.3	19.4
Yorks & Humberside	126.3	47.0
Wales	307.3	38.7
East Midlands	74.5	13.5
West Midlands	108.55	18.7
East Anglia	12.2	4.6
South West	193.5	89.7
South East	149.5	28.8

870.0 (=2,088,000 acres)

The ratio of land to population is, from country to country around the world, anything but uniform. When its population was increasing rapidly between 1500 and 1900, the West appropriated to itself most of the vast open spaces of the earth and built a world system aimed at perpetuating them for the Euro-American peoples.

Table 1
Worldwide Distribution of Land to Population

	Land (1,000 km²)	% of world	Population* (millions)	% of world
White-controlled areas				
Europe	4,929	3.632	523.6	12.4
U.S.S.R.	22,403	16.508	261.2	6.2
U.S.A.	9,363	6.899	218.4	5.2
Canada	9,976	7.351	23.6	.6
Latin America	20,553	15.146	347.2	8.2
Australia	7,687	5.664	14.4	.3
New Zealand	269	.198	3.2	.1
South Africa	2,045	1.507	27.7	.7
Israel	21	.015	3.7	.1
Total	77,245	56.925	1,423.0	33.8
Asian areas				
China	9,561	7.045	914.1	21.7
Southeast Asia^b	1,718	1.276	161.3	3.8
India	3,268	2.408	643.9	15.3
Japan	370	.272	114.0	2.7
Indonesia	1,492	1.099	136.0	3.2
Other^c	11,113	8.197	394.5	9.4
Total	27,522	20.297	2,363.9	56.1
Africa (less S. Africa)	28,179	20.764	422.5	10.0
Oceania (less New Zealand, **Indonesia**)	2,751	2.014	4.7	.1
Total	30,930	22.778	427.2	10.1
World total	135,697	100	4,214.1	100

Notes: (a) As of mid-1978. (b) Countries included: Vietnam, Philippines, Thailand, Malaysia, Laos, Singapore, Brunei. (c) Does not include figures for Kampuchea (Cambodia).
Source: *World Bank Atlas*, 1979.

will also be called for. Nor is there at present any advice or guidance widely available for those taking this leap into the dark.

There is thus no great incentive for an increase in output of organic produce, and a built-in time-lag even for those who decide to make the move in order to satisfy their own moral or environmental imperatives. In particular, such conversion is not even remotely likely on any land which has been intensely cropped for arable farming or for horticulture; beause such land is likely to need a long period of dressings with farmyard manure - which may not even be readily available in the area, particularly from stock guaranteed not to be receiving minerals or medicaments also banned from organic farms - before a sufficient level of organic matter is built up in the soil to support tolerable yields without 'artificial' inputs. The essence of the organic farming system, both for soil fertility and weed and disease control, is the rotation. The grass break grazed and manured by animals, allowed to build up a good level of plant material and then ploughed in, is a vital part; and the fact that only a half or at most two thirds of the farm will be cropping at any one time means that, even if yields are near those of conventional farming, and even with a premium, basic income must be lower.

At present, as far as is known, barely 2,000 acres (well under 1,000 hectares) of land are growing organic vegetables. Even though some of the farms in the process of conversion are of 100 to 300 acres - a larger size than the original smallholder pioneers - the pace of increase is bound to be painfully slow. At present, 60 per cent of the organic produce handled by the still-rudimentary distribution system has to be imported: not least because of the inability of small producers to maintain the year-round supply and the quality required by the supermarkets. And that is where the centre of the argument rests. Four supermarket chains now control over half of all food retailing in this counntry. It is they who set the tone, the standards and the prices for the food production industry. So far, only Safeway, the smallest of the four, has adopted a policy of continous stocking of organic produce. Now and for the foreseeeable future, 60 per cent of that produce has to be imported.

Interestingly, a large proportion of those imports come from Holland. The Dutch have always set the pace and put the pressure on our horticultural industry; and the move to organics is doing nothing to change that situation. In any case, even with unlimited supplies, the retailers' current estimate of the level at which demand may level off is not more than 10 per cent of total fresh produce turnover. Not enough, it must be said, to win an election. In cash terms, that means a total market worth around £13million in supermarkets and perhaps £34million nationally. In 1985, the organic industry, including imports, sold barely £1million's worth of produce.

So it is neither partisan nor dismissive to repeat that the organic sector is not yet within sight of being a significant factor in the total food market; and anyone who bases hopes of reorganising agriculture or land use on that structure is trying to balance angels on the head of a pin. The Green party, by making such a prescription the main manifesto plank of its agriculture policy, demonstrates both technical ignorance in its own field and political inexperience. Indeed, at least one of the major retail chains has declared it has enough problems in organising its conventional supplies without wasting scarce resources chasing the extremely limited supplies of organic produce. Further, it has to be said that the major retailers carry out their own rigorous market monitoring; and tests by several of them on organic produce signally failed to bear out any of the claims of faith that organically-grown produce has a longer shelf life or a taste perceptibly better by consumers than conventionally-grown fruit or vegetables.   This may also point to a much larger problem. While the public may emotionally or subsconsciously lean towards the belief that modern farming is unnatural, destructive of the countryside, and yields produce of lower quality, when it votes with its hands, it faces in the other direction. Such is the demand for vegetables and fruit that are visually perfect and bug-free that buying habits exert enormous pressure to continue with agrochemical use. The average supermarket lettuce receives no less than 14 sprays in its 40-day growing life: and if it did not, the grower would be in real danger of losing his contract with the store, and thus his livelihood. With apples and pears the same applies. Whatever the quasi-religious beliefs of the television and serious newspaper food commentators, people will not buy apples with maggots in them, or lettuces with slugs or caterpillars. If any customer bought a pack of frozen peas with pea moth grubs in it, he or she would immediately call in the Environmental Health Officer. And so purely cosmetic spraying continues, and will do so. Where, above all, the organic movement can begin to make a contribution - and it is only a beginning of a very long process - is in challenging this status quo, and starting to educate people into more realistic and robust buying habits.

The situation with animal products, including meat, is equally difficult. Popular feeling has brought about an EEC ban on growth promoting implants in beef cattle without either any understanding of the magnitude of their dose or effect, or any attempt to distinguish between a number of biologically quite distinct substances. The fact that some are non-hormonal, and the fact that application techniques have become so refined that the actual levels of hormone in the animal's system are far lower than those naturally occurring in young children or indeed in cabbages, go unheard. What is being expressed is not a rational objection to a health hazard, but a fundamental mistrust of science - which expresses itself in the flight from science subjects in school sixth forms, and has been part of the social snobbery of this country ever since Dissenters were excluded from politics and had to go into the 'low' occupations of industry and commerce. A recent Sunday newspaper article on the attitudes of Oxford undergraduates listed the most damning possible description of one of their fellows as "He's a Northern chemist."

The fact that the compounds which, recklessly used in uncontrolled situations on the Continent, produced gross effects in human consumers, have been banned in this country for some time, and without any instance of their misuse having occurred here, is equally disregarded: what matters is that they are regarded as not natural. A similar reaction led to the banning of cyclamate, a non-sugar sweetener of great use for diabetics, simply because massive doses had produced cancer in experimental rats. No experiments administering equally massive doses of sugar to small animals have been conducted, because sugar is 'natural'; although there is virtually no doubt it would be equally lethal. The latest non-sugar sweetener, aspartame, has been introduced with a different public relations approach, which included publicising the one, statistically small risk of its affecting children with one rare condition. There is little doubt that, as a chemical, it offers as little or as much danger as either sugar or cyclamate - or indeed aspirin, which has been linked by different trials to another rare childhood syndrome, and to a protective effect against heart disease. The point noted is not the scientific evidence, which few feel able to assess, but an irrational longing for what is 'natural'. The longing itself is indeed natural; but the thing longed for is frequently highly synthetic - as synthetic as the vision of simple, healthy country life used to sell margarines which are themselves a highly-sophisticated chemically-catalysed industrial product.

This then leads to the further concept of a 'natural' life for the animals that most of us still eat. The example of free range eggs will serve as a useful instance. At present these are able to command up to a 50 per cent premium over normal battery-produced eggs. As a result, a deliberate trial has been carried out at the National Agricultural Centre Poultry Unit to assess the performance and the economics of both systems, as well as the third, deep litter possibility. In year one, the system was very successful, and showed a healthy profit. Laying rates averaged 277 eggs per bird/year, and a profit of £10 per bird was shown, which would be enough to allow an enterprise to support itself.

However, in the second year, performance plummeted. Apart from the loss of 40 birds to foxes, laying rates fell disastrously, and 150 other birds were lost through cannibalism. Further losses arose due to diseases, some of which have not been seen since hens were first moved indoors 20 years ago. Vent gleat became common; infectious bronchitis with the attendant whiter-shelled eggs (again a consumer deterrent), which has been almost completely controlled in commercial layers, reared its head again; and, as time went on, and the ground became hen-sick, the birds suffered from an increasing burden of worms and intestinal parasites. This is natural farming with a vengeance: and it could lead straight back to the Middle Ages.

Nor is any of this special pleading. The fact that, so far, organic or additive-free meat has not become available on the market on any significant scale points to the sheer physical difficulty of organising its supply: and to our lack of any significant body of experience in such production methods. More importantly, it also points to the fact that we have actually placed other priorities first. For instance, if a meat pie or sausage manufacturer is buying supplies of raw material, he will already be working to very tight specifications on such things as bacteriological control levels and fat content. If he were to add freedom from antibiotics, he would be imposing an unpoliceable supply problem on his wholesaler. One of the most progressive supermarket chains has just written to its suppliers asking them to start drawing up a list of their source producers, with details of feeding regimes and husbandry systems, so that at some point in the future they have a data base which could make possible a move in the direction of tighter production control. But at present, the only way to be sure that the meat you eat is completely 'additive-free' is to rear and kill it yourself; or buy it from one of the few very small postal suppliers who advertise in health food magazines. And it has to be said, that is absolutely a minority taste; and a length of trouble that the vast majority of consumers are not at all likely to go to. The task of educating and altering public taste and demand still has far to go.

In the end, any large-scale move in this admittedly attractive direction will depend on market economics. If the producer can satisfy a growing demand while still surviving in business, without being destroyed by better-geared and less-scrupulous competition (usually from abroad), then he will. But any substantial shift in this direction will have to be first demanded by a powerful body of consumer opinion, and then endorsed from the top: and that means, unavoidably, from Brussels. When grants and subsidies are offered to farmers to adopt specified production methods; or when agreed or popularly-demanded restrictions on methods disapproved of are imposed even-handedly across the Community, the move will come. Until then, it will be a matter for a few lonely pioneers who proceed more out of personal conviction than hard-headed commercial enterprise. And what is more, the public, which would not accept such restrictions' being imposed on its own livelihood, will only buy their produce as long as it can afford and until it sees something which attracts it more.

It is a reconstruction of all these attitudes and systems that is needed: for as long as farming is conducted on a so-called 'pure economic' basis, a rational and sustainable land use will not emerge. The present dog-eat-dog system will continue, nationally and internationally. It is a matter of greater urgency than most people realise to arrive at an inventory of the world's resources and a rational distribution of their use and enjoyment. The serviceable area of the earth's surface is at present dwindling, through misuse, at the rate of 200,000 square kilometres a year. In 1980, there were 2 hectares of space for each human being. By 2089, if present trends of population growth and land destruction continue, the human species will have ceased to be viable.

Inescapably, such rationality will be founded on the use of renewable, not exhaustible, resources, and the treating of land as one of those not-inexhaustible resources. Already, the first signs of awareness of this need are being seen in the consuming public. To overcome the powerful momentum of the present economic system, however, will require action from government -or, in the case of the EEC, from Brussels. And that will only come when it is demanded from the grassroots of society: because they have understood where their true interests lie. It would in fact be legally possible, under the Treaty of Rome, for the British government to refuse to accept imports from within the Community on ethical grounds related to production method: but it is almost inconceivable that any government would have the courage to do so. It is only when a broad consensus - of which the beginnings are already visible - of opinion across the whole EEC demands it, that the move will come.

Until that consensus is founded in an understanding of the workings of the economic system, and the land use and agricultural production habits it produces, the change will not be consistent or truly effective. When it does happen, it will necessarily entrain wide-ranging changes in our relations, not only with our own domestic environment, but with the rest of the world: changes which involve not only more sensitive use of natural resources, but more just relations between people and countries. To imagine this will ever happen may be dismissed as naive idealism: but without such idealism, ultimately, we all shall perish.

CHAPTER 8 FORESTRY: SEEING THE TREES AND THE WOOD

There is one crop that will definitely not be in surplus at the end of the century, either in Europe or in the world as a whole. That crop is timber. And while an area of the tropical rain forests equal to half that of Great Britain disappears each year - 5 million hectares (12 million acres) of it primarily into the maw of the Japanese and South Korean building board industries, without, in many places, any effective re-planting policy -world demand for wood pulp and constructional timber as a whole continues relentlessly upwards, whichever forecast we consult.

Unlike energy, for which the demand can be sharply revised downwards either by conservation policies or by a rise in the market price, timber has a basic, indispensible demand level which is fairly directly related to population. and since world population is not likely to level out until the end of the first quarter of the next century, the appetite for timber is virtually certain to continue on up with it. Even if the world economy grows at a very low rate for the rest of the 1980s, the actual material demand for timber is bound to increase: not least because 80 per cent the world's population depends upon it for 80 per cent of the basic necessities of heat and cooking. Of the destruction of the tropical rain forests, far more than the area cleared by commercial logging falls to landless or dispossessed peasants' need for fuel and land to cultivate. This, plus the very long time needed to increase supply - it is not like planting another field of wheat -and the near-certainty of a fall in the value of sterling as North Sea oil runs out, gives forestry a strong comparative advantage, against the subsidised production of agricultural surplus commodities. It may also allow it to hold its own as the source of an expensive raw material, with some industrial investment which would otherwise be heavily import-dependent for its lifeblood.

Forest planting in Great Britain in recent years has taken in 25-30,000 new hectares (60-72,000 acres) per year. Estimates by both the Forestry Commission and the Centre for Agricultural Strategy suggest that this could at most be doubled to 60,000 hectares (144,000 acres) per year . A study by the Energy Technology Study Unit at Harwell has calculated that, after taking into account all restraints on land use - areas protected for scenic and ecological reasons, water supply considerations and other more economically-commanding agricultural uses - a total of nearly 819,000 hectares (1,965,600 acres) are technically available for timber as an energy crop.

Even the well-managed, constantly-renewed resources of the northern hemisphere lumber industry will be outrun by demand; and on broad economic grounds, the case for increased planting in this country seems almost unanswerable. At present we import 90 per cent of our timber needs; and are among the three most lightly-forested countries in Europe - the others being Ireland and the Netherlands.

The forest industry provides one of the clearest examples of the clash between economic reality and woolly fantasy which characterises much of the land use debate. By definition, the timber industry - particularly for wood pulp - is large-scale in its economics and organisation. To imagine that Britain's timber needs can be satisfied by the cultivation of individual fields or small plots in corners of farms, picturesque woodlands, or by an expansion of eco-forests, displays a truly urban, unrealistic view of land economy. To imagine that such a course would even be viable or able to continue without rapid collapse, it is necessary to be living in an imaginary paradise: and one which precisely demands the cushion of middle-class wealth to allow it. Small-scale field-corner, or even field-size forestry will never be more than a hobby, or at best a minor member of a mix of enterprises on a farm unless it spreads to become an essential part of EVERY farm: and thus part of the national landscape pattern. Even in Finland, whose average farm size is similar to ours, in all but the heavily arable and pig-rearing south-west, two thirds of every farm is normally forested. Twenty-five hectares (60 acres) of arable, mainly growing home-produced fodder for a small livestock enterprise (usually dairy) is normally backed by 50 hectares (120 acres) of forest.

There, the trees are the farmer's bank, his capital reserve. When a young man succeeds his father, he will normally fell some of the mature trees to finance new equipment, machinery, farm development, or simply provide material for new farm buildings. He will also take good care -indeed, be required by the government - to replant and maintain a good age-range in his woods, so that his own son will have the same opportunity when the time comes. In both Finland and Sweden, every piece of land, down to parcels below one hectare where necessary, is classified on the basis of soil fertility, climate and prevailing vegetation. On that basis an assessment of potential production is formed, and the value of that is taxed. Thus, if an owner manages his land well, and achieves more than the projected production, he has made some tax-free income; if he neglects it, he has to pay tax on money he hasn't earned: and thus an incentive for good management is built into the system. A two-armed system, one side stemming from the Ministry of Agriculture, controlling permissions to fell, and holding deposited cash to cover re-planting until the work is carried out; the other assisting the farmer with technical advice and, if necessary, organising thinning, weeding, felling and extraction for him: these husband and administer the national forest asset.

In Britain, we are so far from this well-organised, self-sustaining situation, that a major and sustained initiative would be required to move the cause of forestry forward. Numerous studies have shown that the difficulties of putting together sufficient packages of material to make marketing even cover harvesting and extraction costs, or guaranteeing adequate quality as well as quantity to interest the buyer - or of even finding a market which can use the hardwoods which we have come to regard as typical and indigenous - are almost insurmountable. Indeed, it must be said that the cherished belief that hardwoods are English is in itself something of a wilful self-deception.

In a more peasant scale of agriculture, it may still be possible for the individual farmer in the Dordogne to manage a plantation of chestnuts, and get a useful contribution to his total farm income both from nuts and from thinnings and branches sold for woodblock flooring. But then he has the advantage of a climate which allows him also to produce strawberries outdoors in May, and a still-existent tradition of small specialist sawmills used to handling relatively small parcels of high-quality wood and turning it into high-value product. In Britain, there is not a single mill producing parquet flooring: we import all our needs either from the Continent or the Far East. More shamingly, significant quantities of the good quality oak and beech hardwood that we harvest here actually ends up being exported to Germany for processing because we do not have the capacity.

Again, the larger average size of British farm enterprises - compared with their Continental opposite numbers - has taken British farmers away from the habit of thinking co-operatively - if they ever had it - and a major study funded recently by the Countryside Commission found that the habit of keeping back the best produce to play the market and sell privately to the highest bidder will almost certainly defeat any attempt to put together a co-operative marketing system which might offer some hope of making small woodland sales more viable, or at least allow the development of an industry on the basis of reliable volume and consistency of supply.

Traditionally, farm woodlands were always the interest of the landlord, who made it his responsibility to keep them managed, good-looking and valuable for shooting. The tenant farmer never had to develop a tradition of woodland skill and wisdom: witness the fact that today, in an age of 65 per cent owner-occupiers, roughly half the woodland in England and Wales is in small blocks on farms or owned by local authorities, and not subject to a management plan agreed by the Forestry Commission. Of that, four fifths is virtually unmanaged, neglected, and of low value. To get the farmer thinking in the same terms of woodland as he does of his cereal, potato or sugar beet crop, would require an enormous change of perception, and a major advisory input, as well as an indispensible financial or fiscal adjustment to make the figures of the enterprise add up in any terms that he would understand. What is more, the timber cabbages he would be setting out to grow would be utterly unacceptable to the environmentalists, who would be just as horrified by a field of conifers as a hedgeless wheat prairie.

And, at the end of it all, the quantities of timber he would have to market, unless the majority of his neighbours were also able to offer packages at the same time - which suggests a countrywide extension of farm forestry on a Scandinavian scale - would still make the enterprise a low-grade financial performer, and not in any case support any very steady or resilient industry.

Before any meaningful discussion can be had of forestry or the future of land use in this country, the suburban drawing-room picture of a nation of what Sir John Harvey-Jones, then chairman of ICI, in his 1985 Dimbleby Lecture called "a bunch of people in smocks showing tourists round medieval castles" must be knocked on the head. Britain is not going to revert to a peasant economy, or make her living by chopping and selling firewood, home-made bird tables and garden seats. These may all be pleasant pastimes, hobbies or sidelines, but they are not going to butter the national bread; and to offer them as a panacea for survival, or even for the health of the environment, in the last decade of the 20th century displays a truly monumental naivety.

That Britain has a potential as a timber-producing country is beyond doubt - and has been demonstrated by the fact that the Finns have found it worthwhile to put £100 million into establishing the pulp mill at Shotton. A mill of that size is the minimum unit to be viable as an enterprise and capable of competing in the international market. Anything smaller would rapidly find itself without a market because British pulp product users would find imports from other countries more competitive. To take root and grow, it really needs to increase its capacity in the next five years from 450,000 tonnes to 650,000: and that means to be sure that new planting has gone ahead which will guarantee a sufficient flow of material to ensure that large capital investment is fully occupied and earning its keep. That is, in Wales at the rate of at least 3,500 hectares (8,400 acres) a year until the year 2,000. Last year it was a mere few hundred hectares.

The choice as far as timber is concerned is between taking part, or not taking part, in the world industry. If we are to do so, there are no questions about how it can be done. Just as a coal industry involves unsightly spoil tips and ugly pithead buildings, and we accept these because we need the fuel: so a timber industry capable of capturing even a part of our own market and thus releasing us from total dependence on other suppliers, will involve plantation forestry. And to think that, because we still have some of the North Sea oil revenues still left to squander, we shall permanently be able to afford to indulge a privileged taste for small-scale gardening, or make a living out of pheasant shooting, is blinkered foolishness.

To build up and strengthen the multiple-producer farm forestry sector is certainly a possibility: but one which will require a far more complex, lengthy and many-pronged campaign of advice, grant aid to see farmers over the initial 20 to 25-year establishment period, and systematic education in the use of appropriate technology to add value to the crop produced. Also a purposeful fostering of appropriate marketing and processing services.

The point which has so far escaped all inexpert thinking on the subject of timber production, is that an industry cannot be conjured into existence overnight. The reason why farm-scale forestry works in Sweden and Finland is that they already have a substantial national forest asset which guarantees a steady, ongoing supply of material. For Britain to get into that position would require a sustained programme of planting over 30 years until the forests first came into production. If timber, even in 50-hectare blocks, covers half of the land surface of a country, all things become possible. National organisation for management, taxation, harvesting and processing, can exist and function. But to join that club at this stage of the proceedings requires a truly substantial input. A size of input that is not going to be organised on a voluntary or individual farm whim basis.

Britain is not a heavily-wooded country: and has not been for more than two millennia. Oliver Rackham's meticulous analysis in "Ancient Woodland" showed that the level of woodland cover recorded in Domesday was almost certainly little greater than we behold today. The major part of the island's primeval tree cover had been cleared by our Bronze Age ancestors and the Romans; and the "forests" which we are told covered a large part of the land in the time of Robin Hood and Richard the Lionheart were more areas reserved for Royal hunting than stands of densely-packed trees.

Moreover, while slow-growing oak and beech may have been adequate in the days when a population of 5 million only needed them for framing houses and some small shipbuilding, and the faster-growing alder, hazel, willow and birch have satisfied the demands of those days for fuel wood, wattles and hurdles, they certainly cannot satisfy the needs of a population of 56 million. Even in the 18th century, landlords had to impose very precise covenants on tenants, only allowing hedges to be but once in seven years (to ensure an adequate supply of firewood) and only laid the year before corn was sown, to protect it from livestock. Such labour-intensive management by coppicing may be interesting and ideal for the preservation of a historic ecology, but they must be recognised as just that - a special investment in conservation, not an economic activity. The exception is energy coppice -the cultivation of fast-growing species such as willow and hazel for frequent harvest as fuel chips - and that, too is a technique only just being established with, so far, no very convinced government funding or backing.

None of which is to decry the proper management of broadleaved woodlands within our present farm system. There is indeed more than enough to be getting on with if even those already existent are to be rejuvenated and brought back into good order. Moreover, in the process, significant and useful contributions can be made to the farm economy. Woodland work will normally fit into the natural troughs in the year-round workload; cleaning, thinning and coppicing if appropriate will produce useful quantities of wood which, if properly prepared and marketed - even at the roadside - can bring sensible returns. But even here a deal more professionalism is required. At present, as the wood-burning stove industry knows to its cost, most firewood suppliers work to the 'load' - a completely undefined weight and quantity -and make no distinction between the value of a trailer-full of wet, unsplittable elm and a pickup full of useful, ready-to-burn beech or ash.

A few more demonstration farms run by people who have actually learned the skills of preparation, drying, presentation and marketing, and can properly cost the firewood enterprise, would do wonders for this aspect of farm diversification. The proper integration of woodland management into agricultural college courses would do even more; and even ensure that, in 50 years' time most farms would have a number of maturing, high-value trees together with an established fuelwood enterprise as part of their economy.

This, the broadleaf sector, is the aspect of improving overall farm efficiency by maximising activity in an at present neglected area: which would also have the beneficial result of improving a key part of the rural environment both from the point of view of ecology and that of appearance. To catch on, it will demand the development of a more efficient and flexible marketing network and processing industry for hardwoods. The latter might be expected to arise naturally with just a few incentives or grants to encourage new enterprise. The former will almost certainly depend on a major input of exhortation, animation and finance to set up possibly computerised market information networks and develop their executive arm through contractors who will actually carry out the management, extraction, collection and collation of timber in a way which assured both supply to the processor and realistic returns to the grower. It is likely that the grant-encouraged establishment of a hardwood processing/value-adding industry, with its own collection arm which farmers knew would pay fair prices because it depended on a continuing good relationship with suppliers, would do much to encourage woodland owners to gear up their management. If set up in an area surveyed and known to have a sufficient basic tree population of the right species and quality, such an enterprise could transform the situation in a few years. So much for the pretty and parochial, farm-scale side of woodland management. But what of the national-scale, import-substituting aspect? It has to be said that Britain actually has an excellent climate for tree growth. On strict climatic/botanical grounds, these islands are at least partly in the conifer belt; and by temperate standards, are capable of exceedingly good growth rates: some 12 to 16 cubic metres of wood per hectare per year, compared with a Scandinavian average of about 3 cubic metres, and a Canadian one of 1. In Oxford University's Bagley Wood, its Forestry Institute scientists have found that yields up to 18 cubic metres are possible with Corsican pine, or 12 to 16 with the slightly less-productive Western red cedar or spruce. This is on the characteristic heavy clay soil of the area, which is, again, ideal for tree growing because free from moisture stress in all but the most droughty years. And, it is pertinent to point out, it is precisely such heavy soils, capable neither of the top range in arable production, nor of supporting grazing stock for as many months as the better-drained ones, which are most marginal, and most likely to be looking for better use as arable agriculture contracts. On both agronomic and economic grounds, they are entirely appropriate for a lowland expansion of forestry. The question is, will such an expansion be blocked by 'conservation' interests, perhaps better described as preservative attitudes.

If they are, it is as well to spell out the true implications, which are both selfish and obscurantist. They are that it is all right for other countries' environments to be exploited, changed, even destroyed in order to supply our needs; but that ours must not. Other people can live with conifers, but we won't. Pine and birch forests are all right and 'natural' in foreign countries like Sweden or Finland, but we are used to having oaks, ashes and the like on our postcards, and that's all we want... and if a bit more of the tropical rain forests have to be destroyed, or we have to become dependent in yet another way on the United States, in order to balance the world's timber budget, so be it, so long as England stays green and pleasant. The position, stated honestly thus, is surely not tenable.

However, if we can get over the initial hump of accepting that a substantial extension of tree planting on lowland is the most logical and appropriate - and to all but the most change-resisting mind, if undertaken on a site-specific and informed basis, ecologically suitable - use of the 150,000 hectares (360,000 acres) that the National Farmers' Union itself has estimated may need to be taken out of agriculture each year for the next decade, then it becomes possible to discuss the details of management which allow real choices to be made, other than that of the ostrich with its head in the sand. Above all, these are choices about planting density, timber quality, length of growth cycle, species mix and scale of processing.

In many Scandinavian forests - and indeed originally in many in Britain too - pine and silver birch happily combined, the one acting as a nurse to the other, which in due course succeeded it in the rotation. They make an admirably varied forest with wonderful qualities of light and an interesting botanical understorey. The handling and use of the timber produced depends on having a range of industries developed to maximise its value. Denmark, for instance, has a birch flooring industry; birch is a major material of the plywood industry in Finland; and the Finns have made considerable advances in the technique of incorporating birch into the pulp mix for some papers.

The advances made by the Forestry Commission in large plantations, of mixing areas of different species to give variety and enhance topography and landscape, have gone a long way to answer the complaints of insensitivity in earlier mass-afforestation. The requirement that the typical fauna of a given area must not be allowed to change, is, frankly, unhistorical, not to say unnatural. It also ignores the fact that it is perfectly possible to make provision within commercial planting to conserve wildlife habitats by keeping open areas with graded edges and adequate light and species mix.

Even from a tree-growing point of view, the choices are considerable. While planting rates for pine of around 2,500 trees per hectare (6,000 per acre) - as, for instance, in Thetford Forest - are normal in this country, on the Luneberg Heath in Germany, 10,000 (24,000) is the minimum, and some areas go up to 40,000 plants per hectare (96,000). The result is that the individual trees grow a great deal more slowly, the rotation is extended from our 60 years to perhaps 250 years: at the end of which they will have some extremely high-quality timber fit for joinery rather than just sawlogs and pulp. It is a matter of management choice.

What impedes that kind of rational and flexible choice-making in Britain is once again the old demon: the obsession with considering forestry as an investment. Discussion of the forest industry is almost invariably conducted in terms of net discounted revenues which, as often occurs when accountants' nostrums are applied to enterprise and natural systems, produces effective nonsense, or at least a narrowing and impoverishment of activity and opportunity.

On the Continent, net discounted revenues hardly enter into forestry thinking: the whole system is geared towards the highest quantity of the highest value product at the end of the rotation. The kind of "creaming" activity that went on in Britain during the war - taking out the best trees and leaving the rubbish, rather than thinning, taking a few good stems and saving the best to grow on for the final crop - is virtually unknown. The insistence here on wide spacings to obtain maximum growth rate, and four rotations in the time the Germans take for one, helps to produce trees with wide growth rings and thus poor-quality timber only fit for pulping or at best low-grade sawnwood. It also helps to get hardwood growing dismissed as a nonsense because it thinks solely in terms of land cost and area planted. Thus, if oaks are planted on low-grade sandy soil where they are subjected to moisture stress, half the trees may on felling prove to be 'shaken', with internal damage which devalues timber that took 120 years to grow from £100-300 per cubic metre to around £20, the enterprise is obviously disqualified from consideration on accountants' terms, or indeed on farmers'. Similarly, the greater management problems of lowland forest may make them less attractive for the big industrial concerns: the much heavier need for weed control to stop grass and bracken from smothering the young plants; the need for a sustained trapping programme every spring to prevent squirrels from gnawing bark, eating out lead shoots and deforming tree growth; the mounting problem of damage by roe deer; all appear on the negative side of any balance-sheet analysis, particularly as long as land costs remain high.

Until amenity is able to become a significant income generator, the crude logic of business economics tends towards precisely the most insensitive planting, clear-felling and re-planting methods which most outrage the protectors of landscape and ecology. This has without doubt greatly strengthened the current pressure for broadleaf planting versus conifers, which has now produced the Forestry Commission's Broadleaf Woodland Grant Scheme. Even here, emotional rather than rational factors are uppermost: in France, which enjoys growth rates not significantly better than ours, the broadleaf-growing industry is far better-organised, simply because they take a pragmatic, longer-term view of the job - and already have a rotation established. While British commercial planters tend to dismiss broadleaf species because they have only one third the productivity (5 to 6 cubic metres/ha/year) and up to twice the length of rotation (120 years for beech, although only 60 to 80 for sycamore, ash and cherry), the French are geared up to replant steadily as they fell, and are prepared to wait for a high-quality product at the end of the rotation. In Britain, both beauty and a slower-growing higher-quality timber are regarded as luxuries which must be left to the amateur, the enthusiast and the crank. And who can blame those groups for having cranky ideas and altogether eschewing economic considerations, when economics are so narrowly-defined by the 'experts' and professionals?

The whole system is expressed, and skewed by, the way that financial incentives are organised in this country. We have, indeed, grants towards roughly one quarter of the heavy initial costs of planting: but the major incentive for investment in forestry is just that: an investment incentive. To be brief, it consists in tax relief on the other three-quarters of that start-up cost. This automatically makes investment in forestry extremely attractive to people paying the top income-tax rate of 60 per cent. If they can buy land cheaply - and at an extreme we are talking about tracts of the Scottish Highlands not 'cleared' for planting going for as little as £25 a hectare (£60 an acre) - clear and plant it, cover nearly half the cost of doing so out of tax relief and collect another quarter in grant, they can then sit on an asset bought for 30 per cent of its market value; sell it to an institution after about ten years and pay Capital Gains Tax on the land, but not the trees, and still make a handsome profit without ever even going to set eyes on their investment.

Such fiscal measures also encourage new planting rather than wise management of established woodland, factory forests rather than landscape-sensitive woodland: and, above all, they are very little encouragement to farmers, comparatively few of whom actually pay tax at 60 per cent. Their cost to the Exchequer is not very great - one recent official guess put them between £10 and £15 million a year - and their benefit to the British countryside virtually non-existent. They are, once again, part of the panoply of measures reinforcing the hold of wealth on the land: in fact, basically a mechanism for enabling taxable income to be converted into untaxed capital.

Both the objects, of achieving a significant and wide-ranging increase in the woodland cover of this country, and of ensuring that it takes place in a manner reasonably sensitive to the landscape, require the same things. Firstly, that financial incentives be tied to the actual working and productive value of the land, NOT to its capital or speculative value. Secondly, a major and serious attempt to organise education and extension to equip ordinary farmers with the understanding and the skills of woodland management and marketing. At present, farmers as a group mistrust the Forestry Commission, on the grounds that its purchase and use of upland ground has been insensitive, not thinking to spare the patches of better-quality in-bye land that could still have supported livestock enterprises. In fact, if afforestation is sensitively carried out taking cognisance of other farming activity, both forestry and a range of other rural enterprises can benefit, by sharing shelter, roadways and a general improvement in productivity.

There is a place - and an undeniable need - for large-scale planting if any sort of real timber industry is to survive and function in this country. There are powerful arguments for creating situations where the massive resources of the pension funds and institutions, even greater than those of the government itself, can be attracted into forested land, to release the money originally tied up in their creation for further planting. Institutions, after all, never die, never have to pay inheritance tax on long-lived assets, and are thus far better quipped to carry the financial load of industrial forestry.

Probably the Forestry Commission is the best agency to carry this process forward; the most likely to be able to accommodate sensible modifications of planning and planting to take macro-environmental concerns into account. But to do that, it must be allowed to retain and re-use the capital from selling off its already-established forests, not merely asset-stripped and milked, as is currently the case.

This is the first arm of a national forestry policy: the only one likely to make any dent in import need within our lifetimes. The second is an expansion of commercial farm forestry, which is more complex, will start more patchily, but can, with a will - and, above all, consistent all-party fiscal, support and management policies sustained despite changes of government over a half-century or more - be built up into a visually and economically important part of the life of the land. Some suggestions of what those policies might be will be found in the penultimate chapter of this book.

The possibilities of agroforestry - where trees are planted at their probable final harvest spacings, and will thus grow rapidly and produce a good contribution to the land's total return, while another, cropping or livestock enterprise makes maximum use of the space in between - are only just beginning to be explored. Probably our damp, cloudy climate is not ideally suited for such systems: but an increase in the traditional kind of planting of small woodland blocks specifically for timber or fuel is entirely likely.

To administer and facilitate this kind of development, the agency farmers already know and have confidence in - ADAS - will need to combine with the already-existent research and advice facilities of the Forestry Commission. They would not only, with their combination of experience of working with farmers, properly-qualified staff and information back-up, be able to help with the planning of a richer mix of enterprises on the farm, but also to co-ordinate much-needed research and breeding programmes to improve tree productivity in the same way as has already been achieved in arable crops. Estimates suggest a potential 20 per cent increase in timber productivity if breeding and selection were pursued determinedly, particularly in some of our poorer-quality hardwood broadleaves.

The place of forestry in a national structure of family farms has alrady been demonstrated and proven in virtually every European country apart from these islands. The Mansholt Report in the 1960s, in its strategy for the rationalisation and strengthening of European agriculture, recommended the removal of very large areas of land from farming at that time for tree planting. Had it been done, we might well have avoided the huge costs of farm surpluses which are now demanding drastic and precipitate action. The short-sighted pursuit of sectional interests prevented it from happening then. Perhaps, with a will and some imagination, Britain could give a lead where the development of lowland farm forestry is concerned. While some change would be inevitable from the countryside we are used to, an increase on that basis of a million and a half hectares (3.6 million acres) in woodland cover would surely be both a strengthening of our economy and a quickly-accepted enrichment of the landscape.

This is where we return once again to the choice that confronts all discussion of the way forward for the British countryside. Surely it will be better to try to devise an acceptable way of continuing to run a countryside whose principal aim is the production of the means of life, than to forswear all attempt to make a living, run an economy, and confine ourselves to running a fascinating rural museum dependent for its living on nostalgia, scientific study and record-keeping, and tourism. Indeed, if we do the latter, shall we be able to sustain the costs of the attempt? If we do the former on our lowlands, may it not be bearable to accommodate quite sufficient amounts of commercial forestry actually to help supply the national timber need and maintain a viable processing industry, without an unacceptable loss to the total ecology of the country?

Having so done, we should have introduced a new, dynamic, enterprise, new skills, and a new and durable financial base into the farming enterprise, which would help create a ground for the richer, more varied rural life and economy - based on inter-dependent family holdings - that is the basis of a healthy society.

CHAPTER 9 THE THIRD WORLD: A DARK MIRROR

The present world economic order cannot survive with its growth confined to the biggest consumers. Something must be put in its place which gives a larger share of resources and more rapid growth to the poorest, whose condition of life is unacceptable to the conscience of mankind. Since the earth's resources are fast being exhausted, the solution does not lie in redistributing surplus stock.

William Clark: Cataclysm

It is instructive to study the situation of the Less-Developed Countries, because they evidence in gross form the same forces as are working on our own agriculture and environment. In many respects, they make overt the forces which in a mature economy like ours are so disguised as often to escape notice: but which actually operate just as relentlessly.

Take, for instance, the following statements about the situation of farmers in Third World countries, culled almost at random from the two most important recent studies of the effects of the Common Agricultural Policy on the LDCs.

"Small-scale tenant farmers and owner farmers face severe problems as a result of being drawn into the market economy. The most important people in a peasant farmer's life are the 'middle-men' - the lorry owner, merchant and moneylender, who are often the same person. They are the most visible part of the power structure which ensures that the peasant stays poor. Behind them are the bankers, buyers and mill-owners."

"A frequent motive for eviction is the rise in land values with 'opening up' of land for highly commercial agriculture." (We call it 'vacant possession premium'.)

"The most powerful people in a rural society are those who have control over the most land."

"In most countries, the centralised administration of scarce resources -both money and skills - has usually resulted in most of them being allocated to a small group of the rich and powerful."

Speaking of a heavy emphasis on increasing production through mechanisation: "The result has been greater production certainly, but for whom? Many rural tenants have lost their plots as landlords have thrown them off in order to mechanise and many seasonal labourers no longer have work."

"In a project where the major result is to increase the productivity of the land, to a very large extent the distribution of direct benefits must reflect the existing land ownership pattern.

"The Green Revolution...is a good example of technical inputs introduced into an unequal system of landholding, thereby reinforcing or even increasing the gap between rich and poor people... The change to cultivating the new varieties has involved an exposure to many risks and uncertainties not previously encountered. The hybrid seeds, fertilisers and pesticides must be bought at the beginning of each season, and must be available when required. Enough of the crop must be sold at a sufficiently high price to cover these costs and to leave a margin that warrants the extra risk and effort involved. Those who have no capital to invest in such expenditure... are dependent on credit for their purchases and interest charges must also be covered by the eventual sale of the surplus crop."

"The Green Revolution did not result in overall increased agricultural production or in reduced malnutrition. However, it has accelerated the devlopment of a market-orientated capitalist agriculture. In bypassing the need for structural reform in favour of a technical 'solution' to the problem of agricultural productivity, it has made a genuine land reform even less likely." India now has a food surplus problem of almost the same proportions as the EEC, which even threatens the stability of government: but the poor still starve in the streets.

"The living standards of the cash crop exporting interests, concentrated in the towns, depend on a continuous increase in export production to provide the necessary tax revenue and foreign exchange to sustain their lifestyles. Besides a high level of government support and the use of modern technology, the economic success of export production depends on an abundant supply of low-wage agricultural workers ... which undermines the rural peasantry and creates a class of rural proletarians... The fixation on export agriculture only continues because while harmful to most, it is highly advantageous to the large producers and to the small class of better-off urban dwellers."

If we replace the word "export" with "surplus" in this last quotation, it can be seen to apply quite aptly to the British situation. Under the Common Agricultural Policy, it is invariably the large farmers possessed of capital and a substantial area of land who have been best able to take advantage of the advice, grants, and technical means to increase production. Many of them indeed are urban dwellers, combining farming with political or other business interests; and the whole system has demonstrably served to reinforce their position of privilege. Meanwhile, the small farmer with only a family holding to work on, small collateral, and the need to finance fertiliser, spray and seed input costs, has become increasingly burdened with debt, and is now in many cases being forced to sell off even some of the land he has to reduce his debt burden, or "improve liquidity" as the banks will put it. But that 'liquidity' actually describes the flow of his assets down the drain. Business pundits talk often of the need to monitor cash flow. They seldom refer to the cash ebb which is an everyday part of the small farmer's experience, and to many seems to be becoming an irreversible stream.

As development studies show, this approach to agriculture stems from a fundamentally urban-orientated viewpoint. In developing countries, urban industrialisation is seen as the real source of growth; so that a mere 20 per cent of investment is directed to the agricultural sector, in which 75 per cent of the population is employed, and which produces 45 per cent of gross national output. Further, urban, industrial attitudes are extended to agriculture, so that investment, when made, is directed towards mechanised, high-tech, cash-crop, export/surplus agriculture, to the neglect of basic food production, rural employment, or a livelihood for the majority of the population. Further, it tends to drive the poor off the fertile land and into the interior, or onto poorer soils newly-cleared of trees, which in harsh climates leads to rapid soil erosion, desertification and environmental degradation. Meanwhile, the large plantations of the big farmers become huge empty prairies with little of the human about them.

The parallel in Britain produces not starvation, but the ongoing process of rural depopulation - which at present serves only to swell the numbers of urban unemployed; leaving a damaged and simplified countryside in the hands of a shrinking number of ever-larger farmers. Combining with the lack of jobs in local industry in rural areas, this has produced an overall weakening of the rural economy, making it more vulnerable to the operations of the large urban-based or multinational enterprises.

The syndrome has not reached, and will not reach, the savage lengths here that it displays in many Third World countries: but while the quantity may be different, the quality is the same. A world ruled by self-interest and the raw laws of the market will always be messy, and frequently cruel. What we face in this country, in the current phase of the economic cycle, is an increasing division between a wealthy, insensitive, environment-abrading intensive/big business sector, and a slow but visible increase in poverty, both in personal and landscape terms, in the less-privileged areas. Two kinds of wildness: that of the fat cat, red in tooth and claw, and that of a neglected countryside. Neither is to be recommended: nor is either going to enhance or strengthen those qualities which typify the British countryside at its essential best.

And this wildness has one source: a system in which land and labour are regarded as commodities to be bought and sold. The system that we, as colonisers, imposed on the Third World, and whose costs we still have ourselves to pay. Another quotation is telling:

"Trade structured to drain wealth has been a prime mechanism in under-developing the now poor countries.

MORE OF THE SAME IS NOT THE ANSWER. Trade is promoted uncritically by elites whose control over productive resources allow them to profit by foreign sales at the expense of the majority."

My thesis is that the concentration of wealth, mainly in the form of monopoly control of land, in the hands of a relatively small section of the population has resulted in widespread starvation in less-developed countries. In Britain, attention has been distracted from its action by just over half of the population's being encouraged to indulge in the minor land speculation of open-market home purchase; but it has by the same economic mechanisms, resulted in homelessness, unemployment, and malnutrition for the other slightly less-than-half. The unemployed and the homeless are paying for the comfort of the well-housed and comfortably-paid in this society just as much as starvation in the Third World is the price of the prosperity of the industrialised countries. And while the activities of the robber land barons of north-eastern Brazil, and the plantation owners of East Africa and Asia are easily seen to be wreaking frightening damage on the world's ecostructure, and spawning future mega-cities of shanty-towns hung like boils on a core of skyscrapers, the activities of the business ethos in agriculture and land use, even in our ecologically well-buffered and economically intensely-privileged island, are subtly degrading the environment, and building deprivation and impoverishment into the structure of our society. To encourage a small farmer to take out an overdraft in times of inflating land values, which he can no longer secure or repay when land values and produce prices start to fall; to encourage a developing country when commodity prices are high to borrow to finance grandiose infrastructure which becomes a millstone when the markets collapse; and to lead the council house tenant to take a mortgage in the belief that economic growth will continue, and that having 5 per cent of the equity of his house gives him secure entry to the class of property owners: all these are cruel confidence tricks. Of the three, the second is proving murderous.

In his study of the effects of the Common Agricultural Policy on the Less-Developed Countries, Alan Matthews sets out the whole world situation thus: "There is but one world economy, it is capitalist, and the performance of national economies is determined by their location within the world capitalist system. In conformity with the law of uneven development in capitalist societies, some nations - almost all lying in the northern hemisphere - form the core of this system; the remainder belong to the periphery. The superior performance of the core economies results from the dynamics unleashed by the accumulation of capital - an accumulation that has in significant part resulted from the expropriation of economic surplus from the underdeveloped countries. The underdevelopment of the less developed countries is thus not a prelude to their subsequent development: rather, the peripheral nations remain underdeveloped precisely because they bear and have borne much of the cost of developing the capitalist world."

What we see is the development of a Global Farm supplying a Global Supermarket. And while supermarkets spread a liberal supply of goods across a wider range of the population, it is still only to the part of the population that can afford them. If the CAP were liberalised now, Matthews calculates, it would profit those less-developed countries which export temperate zone commodities, but the higher prices they would receive for their produce would further skew land ownership against the poor; and meanwhile those LDCs which currently export oil/protein meals to our human food and livestock industries would find their markets and income contract; while those who are net importers of food would suffer even more greatly from hunger as we began to compete with them for food from the world market: with the result that the overall effect would be between £0.3 and £1 billion LOSS to the Third World. Ideally, he says, the CAP should probably encourage European cereal production to keep world prices down and offer an alternative source of supply to the USA, while discouraging the production of livestock feed products and sugar - the exact opposite of the Policy's current trend.

Thus have we built the Less-Developed Countries inextricably into the net that supplies our needs. To shop at Sainsbury's for good, clean, additive-free food, one needs a certain income, and probably a car to bring away one's purchases. To live in Britain and be concerned about environmental conservation, one has not only to be among the most fortunate 20 per cent of the world's population, but also to ignore the fact that that abundant and competitively-priced supply of food is the fruit of massive injustice on a world-wide scale, and of a loading of the scales against equal opportunity and a living countryside at home.

Until the marginally-privileged - the middle-class small home-owners, the urban enjoyers of the economic benefits of this system, who are in many cases the same people who swell the conservation movement, realise that they themselves are part of, and profit from this institutionalised injustice, conservation will never be much more than a rather arch and sophisticated game of nymphs and shepherds. In the final chapters I shall try to spotlight the steps that actually need to be taken if health is to be brought back to the countryside and the system as a whole.

CHAPTER 10 THE SOIL TRADE

If one could have a speeded-up film of the British countryside over the past 5,000 years, it would look like a living thing, breathing in and out, pulsating, or like a flower budding, leafing, blossoming, dying back and breaking out into leaf over and over again. Settlements grew up, drifted up hill or from field to be near new road, withered as population fell, the economy faltered or communications changed; or kings, lords and landowners re-modelled their estates.

What was surprisingly constant, from the Stone Age through the Iron Age, the Roman empire, the Saxons, was the basic unit of land: the estate -whether as the base of a community, tribe, family or lord, or simply a unit of agricultural organisation. A remarkable consistency of distance between settlements, of around 4 kilometres/2.5 miles (decreasing on the best land) has been observed over a great deal of continuously-occupied land. Land may have fallen out of use, but when used, there seems to have been a basic viable unit of exploitation. It is only when economic, rather than social or agronomic factors come into play that things change.

Individual farms or villages may have been abandoned, but the basic pattern of settlement, and indeed of major landscape character, has been largely unchanged for centuries. Interestingly, Taylor has found that, while some outlying farms on the edge of Dartmoor were abandoned in the mid-14th century as population and the economy contracted, others no better placed continued in occupation. Painstaking research showed that the crucial difference between them was that the ones abandoned were tenanted farms which, in a contracting economy, ceased to return an economic rent: and so were written off in accountants' terms. Those which survived were freehold farms where the occupants only had to produce enough to live, not to pay rent. The same phenomenon is likely to be seen in the poorer upland areas in the late 1980s, where farming will survive as a way of life because there is no other way available.

The effects of farming on the environment have, similarly, been gentle and organic, producing a particular but constantly-changing ecological balance in a fundamentally fluid situation. The ecology of the Somerset levels, for instance, over which such battles have been fought in recent years, is itself a delicate, labile and almost accidental event produced by what a historian might regard as a momentary pause in an ongoing process of colonisation and intensification of use. As Lowe et al say in their powerful account of the West Sedgemoor controversy, "The past ecology of West Sedgemoor is little known so, paradoxically, most of the reliable wildlife information dates from the period after 1944 when significant and sustained improvement became possible. In any case, it is probable that the winter water-level would previously have been too deep for wading birds so that much of the area's present ornithological interest would not have been apparent then. Today, following an extensive survey, the RSPB regards it as the most important breeding site in south-west England for waterfowl... A high water table keeps many of the soil invertebrates at or near the surface, thereby providing food for the bird populations."

What this makes clear is that the present ecological position, which conservationist concern has, as it were fixed in the freeze-frame of a survey at a particular instant of history and agricultural development, is in itself only one of a thousand different states through which this land has gone, and no doubt will go again in the future: after our civilisation has passed, if not before.

The sense of alarm, of a fragile beauty trembling on the brink of extinction is, I would suggest, more a reflection of our sense of our own fleeting tenancy of this earth, than a rational scientific assessment of the threat to our environment: a scared clinging to a measured status quo -albeit in some cases one only quite recently-created - for fear of facing change. The same spirit as moves district Planning committees to spend endless hours deliberating over specifications of 'traditional' materials for building projects in the countryside, rather than permit any contribution to the rural scene truly worthy of the 20th century. And so we cling in villages to an endless mediocrity of neo-vernacular, and fail to create any living environment which expresses the social relationships, the technical possibilities, or any true confidence in, our own age and stage of English society.

Lest this be taken as a partisan defence of farming interests, it must be said that a similar myopia afflicts the landowner/farmer viewpoint in conservation disputes. The history of the Berwyn makes clear that most landowners take the name Site of Special Scientific Interest to mean a small and specific plot of ground: and to feel that if its size can be whittled down to within sufficient limits, its preservation as a micro-sample of a passing ecological picture can be accepted, and the costs of doing so made supportable. Neither side seems often to grasp the fact that what is being discussed is a broad, living, palpitating landscape stretched over a period of time - during which it will in any case inevitably undergo changes.

The first question that has to be honestly faced is: do we want to fix a specific moment of history exactly as it is, to fossilise one particular accident, or set one particular unstable ecological sub-climax in concrete or amber? And if so, why?

Having answered that, we next have to select which particular instant is the most worthy of such immortalisation, and prepare to face the costs of achieving that end. In general, the environments valued by conservationists are those typical of low fertility and extensive agricultural systems held in a precarious stability by intermittent grazing. They are, to be blunt, typical of a society with a lower level of economic expectations than ours, lesser population pressures, and far smaller democratic expections on the part of its citizens.

Now it may be possible, in the present economic climate, to impose a return to such a society. We have already succeeded in imposing it on some 4 million - nearly a tenth - of the nation by casting them out of work and telling them they are simply helpless victims of historic economic pressures and the second Industrial revolution. But, to achieve the kind of arrest in landscape evolution that is envisaged in some conservation scenarios requires another, and of late far more robustly independent, class of people to accept a sharp reduction in their status and standard of living. When the Wessex Water Authority and the local IDB first proposed in 1977 a million-pound drainage scheme which would virtually eliminate flooding on West Sedgemoor, it was rejected by a majority of local farmers, because they feared the drainage rate could become prohibitive. Their fathers before them had vociferously opposed the introduction of the first pump drain on the moor in 1944. But to ask them today to return to a regime of summer grazing and haymaking, with virtually no winter use of land which has since proved as highly fertile for a range of crops as the Lincolnshire fens, just scratching the rest of their living from fattening beef calves from the dairy herd, is to demand a cut in standard of living which there is no sign of any employed, still less professional, person's accepting - however far it may be in the national interest.

To become a farmer demands in the first place a considerable independence of mind and a determination to be master of one's own fate and enterprise: they are in the habit of thinking and working through problems, and for a generally conservative lot, have a remarkable openness to new ideas. But dictated to, or treated as if still at school, they will not be. As long as agricultural production is the sole source of income generation in the countryside, farmers' reactions to demands for a lowering of intensity to increase conservation are likely to be reluctant or inflexible. If other sources of income become available, the situation opens up.

What it amounts to is that we are discussing whether a major increase in public spirit and self-sacrifice is possible: and whether the community at large is able to accommodate a whole range of new ideas about how the countryside is to live. If the answer to that is "yes", then a whole range of political and economic options suddenly come into discussion.

I personally do not believe that the past can be conserved or the future resisted simply by decree; or that, by creating a set of fossilised, largely-unvisited nature reserves, we shall have struck any meaningful blow for society or the environment. If such areas are within reach of the major centres of population, they will tend to be over-used and thereby eroded and degraded; if far, they will be neglected and irrelevant, unenjoyed by any but a few scientists and pundits.

What is urgently required is an honest examination of the full range of options in our countryside, a clear decision as to how much food we require to produce from it, and what methods of production are acceptable, and a responsible decision to provide for the costs of those choices. Unless farmers are to be forced to relinquish the progress they have made in the social and economic scale, it will be necessary to accept that probably the full amount currently spent on agricultural support be diverted to direct income support for farmers as "landscape gardeners and not as agriculturists", to use the phrase of Professor S R Dennison, in his dissenting report from the Committee on Land Utiisation in Rural Areas as long ago as 1941.

Alone in a Committee chaired by a judge and former vice-president of the CLA, and including in its membership L Dudley Stamp, whose Land Utilisation Survey in the late 1920s had first rung the alarm bells about the rate of loss of farmland to urban sprawl, Dennison had the vision to see that already the rural community was no longer largely agricultural, and that the course of post-war farming would be governed by efficiency, which meant specialist, not mixed, farming, and a considerable shake-out of the agricultural workforce. "He clearly regarded as nonsense the dictum of the Majority Report that 'the cheapest, and indeed the only way, of preserving the countryside in anything like its traditional aspect would be to farm it.' He regarded traditional farming as incompatible with prosperity and was happy to see it disappear."

Today, we have recognised the first part of that truth, but have still to accept the second. Farming purely by the pressures of economics, technical progress, and mass consumer demand, will indeed tend to simplify the landscape and the rural ecological habitat. Putting fragments of it into a Rip Van Winkle slumber will not, however, prevent that change on a meaningful national scale. The only thing that will is radical economic action, calling for a completely new understanding of the motors of the economy, and a willingness on the part of the whole of society to accept personal cost. An indispensible prerequisite of any solution will be that the urban population should be as willing to relinquish some of its privileges, as it asks the rural sector to be. It requires us to go back to the fundamental meaning and value of the land, and re-interpret it for the present day. For that, it is necessary to turn to the early economists and philosophers.

In the 17th century, John Locke first formulated that "as much land as a man tills, improves, cultivates and can use the product of, so much is his property." "Labour is what distinguishes what is privately owned from what is held in common; the labour of a man's body and the work of his hands. Labour is the unquestionable property of the labourer; and by mixing his labour with material objects a man acquires a right to what he has worked on and to what he has made of this material." It is from this basic concept that all our subsequent thinking about private property has grown.

It was the Tory philosopher Burke who first enunciated and developed the favourite term of today's landowners: stewardship. Confronting the rise of utilitarianism - the new capitalists, who did not recognise moral obligation or duty as guides to action, and thus, in his mind, represented a threat to the continuation of a stable social order, he enunciated the concept of stewardship of the land: of a class responsible for its good care and government, building on, but straying some way from, Locke's original thesis, which had dismissed the idea of private property in land at all.

Land, all early philosophers had argued - and all early societies practised - is a product of nature. It is of a fixed amount and is vital to the survival of all forms of life. As Prof Masrui has explained, in uncorrupted African society to this day, land is communally held, and each is guaranteed sufficient for his need. The idea of title to specific plots of land was one imposed by the colonial powers to create a mechanism for its estrangement; and the private ownership of this natural resource has resulted - in our own history, and today on a massive scale in developing countries - in starvation, homelessness and unemploymentfor millions, whilst a tiny minority of very rich and powerful landowners enjoy luxury beyond the imagination of most people.

Marx correctly identified property as the basis of economic and political domination; capital is known by economists as power over the labour of others; but it was left to the American Henry George to point out that there is a difference between the fruits of the individual's labour, and the capital value of land. A distinction which has become increasingly blurred and obfuscated as property ownership has become more widely diffused through society, and been tapped as the motivating power of the political order. "A sense of immutability and inevitably has attached to the distribution of property, especially in the ownership of land, which has become surrounded by a varied set of cultural symbols emphasising continuity", as Newby puts it. The idea of the Englishman's home being his castle has so permeated popular thinking that today, in Oxford, one estate agency has chosen the name Finders Keepers; while a firm which sprays insecticide to eradicate woodworm has renamed itself Heritage Preservation: the sense of possession and maintaining permanence becoming paramount.

All of which has taken us some distance from Ricardo's original concept of economic rent. It was upon this that George - who was far from being a socialist - built his understanding of the proper organisation of society and the economy. According to Ricardo, "the rent of land is determined by the excess of its produce over that which the same application can secure from the least productive land in use." And it is in this, the true economic rent of a piece of land, that the distinction between personal property and the rights of society consists. For example, it is not only the good fortune of being allowed to occupy land of superior fertility which conveys a higher rent or income. The closeness to a major market, the provision of easy transport in the form of a major road or railway, the hundred and one demands which the actions of the community at large generate, all have the effect of increasing the value of a particular site: and none are produced by the individual occupant of it. Merely by occupancy of that site, the landowner is the passive recipient of additional value created by the community and its public expenditure.

In this respect, all land is subject to the same laws: whether agricultural, residential, commercial or industrial; whether urban or rural. The unearned portion of the value of urban land is perhaps more readily demonstrated. Detailed studies have shown that construction of commuter railway lines have had a measurable effect in increasing property values. In Toronto, the construction of the underground system was shown to have caused the prices of adjacent homes to increase by 45.4 per cent, when the whole-city increase was only 32.8 per cent.

In Philadelphia, it was calculated that each dollar's worth of daily transport cost saving added •149 to residential price. The Philadelphia-Lindenwold rapid transit line cost •94million to build and, by this calculation, added •34million to the land values of its customers. The construction of the Docklands Light Railway line in the East end of London will have a comparable effect on land values in Tower Hamlets eastwards - a ten-fold increase has been predicted - and was vigorously lobbied for by the developers as a result. Similar rises in rental and capital value of all commercial property in the Green belt, and corresponding pressure for further development, are already being recorded around the M25 London Orbital motorway.

The government's creation of 'Enterprise zones' where firms can enjoy exemption from rates, many planning controls and training requirements, and 100 per cent capital allowances for industrial and commercial buildings has had two simple effects: firstly, to transfer existing firms from nearby into the zones; and second, quite rapidly to lead to higher rents within the zones as the special privileges became capitalised into land values. Rents in the Swansea zone are now higher than the cost of rentsrates outside it. It has been argued that the enterprise zones have in fact not succeeded in creating any new jobs, and that property developers and landowners have been the only real beneficiaries.

Indeed, it is generally the developer or land speculator who pockets the spin-off profit from public projects: that is, the temporary landowner. The story of the young estate agent Harry Hyams' purchase of a property in Grafton Street, W1, for £59,000 from an owner who could not get a building licence for it, is instructive. Building licences were abolished the next week, and when the vendor enquired if he might buy the property back, was told that the price had gone up to £100,000. The seemingly incomprehensible phenomenon of new office blocks being kept empty for years become instantly understandable when the increase in their capital value as rents rise due to the artificial shortage of accommodation - which far outstrips the interest on their building cost - is divided by the number of years. Centre Point was an 'Intervention Store' in the office accommodation market, as directly financed by the consumer as the wheat, butter and beef mountains of the CAP.

By the same token, the owners of farmland, whether rentiers or owner-occupiers, profit both from public works - the construction of motorways and public utilities, the growth of villages and nearby towns, the construction of airports and the like - which create demand pushing up the price of land they have to sell. One Oxfordshire farmer of my acquaintance used to grow his own barley on 60 acres and feed it through his own 70-sow pig herd to make a living.☎ He is now hoping to sell his farmyard - now in the centre of the village - for a quarter of a million pounds for housing development, and thereby finance the purchase of a further 100 acres of land for cereal cultivation. Using a low-cost system for spring barley, which demands far fewer spray inputs because of the sanitary break over winter, he is confident he can survive on selling his grain to others even if the cereal price comes down to the world level of £80 per tonne.

More importantly, all farmland owners have benefited from the capital grants and guaranteed high market prices for their produce over the past 40 years and, as Body has rightly emphasised, the major part of the benefit has been capitalised into land values. (It is noticeable that, in the manufacturing sector, where labour costs go down, due either to productivity increase or wage restraint, company profits do not automatically increase: what invariably goes up is the value of the land on which the factories and offices stand.)

It is to this point, again and again, that we must return: Land is not just another form of capital, and agriculture is not just another industry. When the capital value of land and farming as an activity become confused, the quality of farming suffers, as does the quality of the farmer's life; and so does the countryside, because the bank is pressing for ever more intensive production.

The actual import-saving value of British agriculture is strictly insignificant in any macro-economic analysis: quite properly and understandably, its value stems from irrational factors like patriotism, the hangover of wartime need for secure food supply. A proper provision against a disastrous harvest which could precipitate world shortages quite unexpectedly, must surely be made. The large areas of agricultural land that could be put out of production by such an accident as Chernobyl showed that quite clearly. On a world-wide scale, it is essential to avoid flipping agriculturally-productive areas into a decline from which they cannot be rescued except by collossal capital expenditure or a very long, slow rejuvenation process. The state of North Africa - once the granary of Rome -is a vast and awful warning which is underlined by each yard the desert advances southwards. The same will not happen here, but change could still be very difficult to reverse, if precipitated without proper consideration. That said, if any clear thinking is to be done on the future of the British countryside, the idea that its sole function is food production must be set on one side. We can, with profit both to ourselves and other nations' producers, obtain what we need elsewhere IF THAT IS WHAT IS BEST.

This is not to say that we should give up the idea of farming in this country, nor even necessarily that our farmers should be exposed to the full blast of international economic competition: simply that, until we unhitch farming from the thrust of land capital values, no sane solution will be found to the questions of agricultural surplus, economic problems and the destruction of the environment. It is the beady eye of the bank - and of other citizens - on the security value of land, which has driven many a farmer to over-extend himself and get onto a treadmill from which there appears no escape. It is to land as a security that the speculator returns again and again: in time of economic blizzard as a safe haven in which to sit and wait it out - which in turn guarantees that the insane spiral of land price inflation will renew itself again.

Farmers are not land speculators. They have far too much

to do to indulge in that kind of semi-criminal activity. But in the way the economic order is at present structured, they have had to learn to play the game of security, borrowing, investment and gambling on their own enterprise; and at present a substantial number of them face an abrupt and painful unhitching through the mechanism of business failure.

This is, however, only a change of horses, unless something is done radically to re-structure the whole system. Land values will fall to the point where it becomes attractive for a new generation of speculator/entrepreneurs to get on the roundabout again. The figures show it happening again and again at roughly 18 year intervals in the urban economy since the late 18th century when the Industrial Revolution first sputtered into life. And each peak in land values has been abruptly followed by a drying-up of industrial investment as the high cost of rents took too high a share of production costs; an economic recession; and a downward adjustment of land values as demand temporarily faltered. That downward adjustment, in human terms, meant bankruptcy not only for the unwiser speculators, but also for numbers of honest and hardworking businessmen. Our task must be to find a way of getting off this endless, sickening up-and-down spiral. If that can be done, the wiser operator will see that a degree of apparent sacrifice will bring far greater benefits than losses.

Hitherto, farmland has acted only as the bank, the reserve to fuel the speculative swings and roundabouts: today, the farming industry has become fully integrated and participant in their most giddy lurches. The remedy, I would suggest, is still that proposed by Henry George in 1870. Marx, because of his concentration on the ideology of class war, gave insufficient weight to the effects of the monopoly of land, although he recognised its existence. George's remedy was simple, elegant and recognised as effective: to tax the economic rent of all land. It is one still recognised as possibly the only effective way of building stability and strength into the economies of the less-developed countries: as Alan Matthews says, "probably favourable prices for produce combined with land taxation is the only way."

Land is the property of the whole of humanity, and cannot belong exclusively to any individual, argued George: an assertion which sounds almost like blasphemy to today's ears, schooled on the sacredness of private property. In his own time, he sounded less revolutionary.

"There is no foundation in Nature, or in natural law, why a set of words upon parchment should convey the dominion of land; why the son should have the right to exclude his fellow-creatures from a determinate spot of ground, because his father had done so before him; or why the occupier of a particular field, when lying upon his death-bed and no longer able to maintain possession, should be entitled to tell the rest of the world which of them should enjoy it after him," wrote Sir William Blackstone in the mid-18th century. John Stuart Mill followed him in the age of Victoria by stating:

"the essential principle of property being to assure to all persons what they have produced by their labour and accumulated by their abstinence: this principle cannot apply to what is not the product of labour, the raw material of the earth.

"When the sacredness of property is talked of, it should always be remembered that any such sacredness does not belong in the same degree to landed property. No man made the land: it is the inheritance of the whole species.

"There are those who think that the land of a country exists for the sake of a few thousand landowners, and that as long as rents are paid society and government have fulfilled their function. But this is not the time, nor is the human mind now in a condition in which such insolent pretension can be maintained. The land of every country belongs to the people of that country."

From this revolutionary utterance of a well-known bourgeois philosopher, let us return to Marx, whose analysis was undeniably shrewd and clear-sighted.

"In so far a commodity production and thus the production of value develops with capitalist production so does the production of surplus-value and surplus-product. But in the same proportion as the latter develops, landed property acquires the capacity of capturing an ever-increasing proportion of this surplus-value by means of its land monopoly and thereby, of raising the value of its rent and the price of land itself... The landowner need only appropriate the growing share in the surplus-value and the surplus-product, without having contributed anything to this growth... the singularity of ground rent is rather that together with the conditions which agricultural products develop as commodities... there also grows an increasing portion of these values, which were created without its assistance; and so an increasing portion of surplus-value is transformed into ground rent."

In farmyard terms, this is saying that, given the basic fertility of the soil, the agricultural output of which it is capable, beyond a certain basic level, is increasingly due to the efforts and inputs made by the farmer - of labour, machinery, fertiliser and good husbandry. But nonetheless, as he increases the output of his farm, so the rent - or the interest payment to his bank or mortgagee - increases: so that the landowner, or the lender who has taken a charge on it, takes a larger share; and the farmer is actually paying rent on his own sweat, materials and skill.

Having brought that fact out into the open, we begin to see the question more clearly. But what about the owner-occupier? Clearly, he is in the position both of tenant and landowner, so that the additional portion of his surplus product attaching to the land is actually increasing the value of his capital holding. It is here that we get onto decidedly stickier ground, to coin a phrase. What is the value of that ever-inflating capital asset?

The answer, ultimately, has to be inheritance. The common and understandable wish to leave something to one's children bedevils the whole question, and until this ticklish and often painful issue is fully examined, no further progress can be made towards a workable solution. Perhaps this urge might be less imperious in a society with more hope and a real sense of forward movement. But if we start by recognising one simple fact, and view it with a degree of humility, progress may be possible. It is obvious that, in a country with 20 million hectares of usable land and 56 million inhabitants, that it is not possible for many of them exclusively to possess a great deal of land without many others having to go critically short. Shared equally, there is about one acre of land per person in this country. Even shared unequally, once a few hundred have over 1,000 acres each, there is not much more than a cupboard or a park bench left for several thousand others. It should be possible to satisfy the need to create and hand on viable family enterprises, and still agree that enough is big enough.

The possession of land is in itself a considerable power, with a built-in ratchet effect. Many a young would-be farmer beholds it in action in his own sphere: when a farm comes on the market, it is the neighbouring farmer, already owning land which can act as collateral to borrow money, who is able to step in and buy it. And so the amalgamation process continues. Moreover, since the pressure of economics dictates that larger holdings are more viable and easily-managed than smaller, competition to secure that extra portion of land in itself helps to push the price up. Until recently, the tax concessions available also built in advantage for the farmer with the larger acreage who could therefore buy larger machinery and claim heavier reliefs; and grant aid was also more oriented towards the larger, more 'efficient' holding.

Then, simply by virtue of holding land, and being able effectively to speculate on it by monopolising the supply, and thereby further forcing up the price, the landowner can further reinforce and entrench his position. Distasteful though it may be, it has to be said that he thereby makes it even more difficult for the landless majority to possess or enjoy any land at all. The ownership and bequest of land is the most powerful mechanism for the transmission of privilege, power and advantage to one's own offspring, and the fixing of disadvantage to everyone else's.

Herein lies the root of a great deal of social conflict. In Bangla Desh, the large landowner tends also to be a money-lender: when the smallholder lacks the funds to buy seed, fertiliser or the means to cultivate his land, the large owner lends to him at exorbitant rates of interest. When it proves impossible to pay the debts and survive, he takes the smallholder's land -and so we have a country with several million landless inhabitants, reduced to working intermittently at desperately low wage rates as labourers on the large landowners' lands. By exactly the same mechanism, the developed countries have lent to less-developed countries, normally to enable them to buy large machinery or invest in major capital projects of a high-tech nature and thus get locked into dependence on material and technical supplies from the advanced economies; and then - or rather, NOW - when interest rates go up and the interest burden on those loans becomes difficult to support, loftily prescribe that the debtor countries' populations should "tighten their belts" until the debt is cleared.

The problem is not the fecklessness of the Third World poor, but the system of land and capital ownership itself, which operates to magnify their disadvantage. The only way of curbing that system is that already introduced to regulate some of our production excesses: quotas. Land reform - A Land Quota system - to spread resources efficiently across the maximum number of effective enterprises, is the answer which cannot forever be ignored: here, as there.

The farmer members of the Milk Marketing Board of England and Wales in 1986, by a historic vote, replaced the "cow vote" which gave larger producers effective dominance, with a one-man/one-vote system. In the councils of world finance and banking, no such just arrangement operates: the majority of votes are held by the richest countries. They are used to perpetuate the systems of land tenure and exploitation that underpin the wealth of the industrialised world's banking system. Last year, it cannot be too often repeated, the total paid by all the African countries in interest exceeded all that they received in 'aid'.

And just as "bigger fleas have smaller fleas, upon their backs to bite them, and smaller fleas have smaller fleas - and so ad infinitum", so the structure of exploitation, always based on land ownership, permeates the whole system. Where, under colonial rule, subsistence farmers and long-established pastoral systems were dispossessed to allow the creation of plantations growing tea, coffee, sugar cane, as cash crops for the settlers' enrichment, today the Westernised elite who took over at independence continue to acquire, accumulate and run large farms producing the same cash crops. The cash system - introduced in colonial times so that the imposition of taxes could force country people out of subsistence farming into wage employment - continues to hold the poor in dependence on the crumbs from the table of a capitalist economy. And while the world market for cash crop commodities is over-supplied and their prices fall lower and lower, they still bring wealth and power to the plantation owners; while the small farmers who formerly occupied the land are reduced to becoming migrant workers, or moving into the towns and cities, visitng their families occasionally and sending them remittances from what work they can find. (They have counterparts in this country in the Cleveland bricklayer forced to leave his family to find work in Surrey because the concentration of the steel and other industries into 'economic' units elsewhere has left his own county unable to support a flourishing building industry.)

In many developing countries, land-holding has disrupted long-standing stable farming systems which formerly maintained the balance of a fragile Nature. Around Lake Baringo, in the semi-arid northern part of Kenya, the Pokot and Njemp tribesmen have been prevented from making their traditional move southwards with their livestock in the dry season by the establishment of cereal and other farms around Nakuru. As a result, overgrazing has destroyed the ground cover, and rains, when they come, cause floods that rush down off the hills, carving deep fissures which have become textbook examples of soil erosion. Desperate stock graze the first flush of grass after rain, before it has time to set and scatter seed, and removing the cover which could ha   ve protected seed from birds. Goats clamber on trees to browse, and the bare soil is progressively washed off into the lake, making it cloudy, reducing fish stocks and evaporation which might feed more reliable rains. The start of all this pernicious process is the reservation of blocks of land for conventional, intensive arable agriculture.

In the cities, the affluent middle classes acquire villas - with high wire fences and askaris (armed guards) - while skyscraper building pushes ground rents sky high in the pursuit of office and shop building. Ordinary small traders are forced to work from stalls or pitches in the streets, and at night return home to the shanty towns in the valleys and on the outskirts. They would find more than a little in common with the unemployed youth who rioted in Brixton, Handsworth and Toxteth for sheer frustration at lack of opportunity.

All these are different manifestations of the same mechanism: young farmers in Britain unable to get started because the key to a farm is a £quarter-million; migrant workers in Third World countries who can no longer scrape a living on their shambas; unemployed youngsters in our cities no longer needed by an economy ruled by the pressure for short-term profits, or industries which find it easier to show such profits from property transactions than by investment in real production and wealth creation; and established small farmers who face bankruptcy as the economic recession knocks the bottom out of their collateral: all are victims of the property vice, the worship of the unearned income of land speculation rather than the genuine value of industry - personal or communal.

Meanwhile, many of the postwar generation of owner-occupier farmers in this country find themselves the object of the envy of land-hungry urban-dwellers, and accused of profiteering when in fact all they are doing is carrying their banks. One of the privileges they are most begrudged, as public services decay due to the cash limits imposed on local authorities, is their exemption from local rates. "They burn their cereal straw, but don't even pay their share of the costs of the fire brigade," is the cry. It may however be that the call for rating of farm land - the foregoing of a privilege earned between the wars by suffering, and long-cherished by farmers -may be a pointer to a more rational organisation of the finances of the countryside. Provided only that the income thus raised is reinvested in the strenthening and invigoration of the rural areas: if it is merely creamed off to a central Exchequer, the rural sector is being still further colonised by the urban sector and its interests. And it is precisely a reversal of that trend that is required to create a healthy environment, both socially and ecologically (and the one depends upon the other) in the countryside.

The first step is to form a clear vision of what is wanted; the second, by appropriate fiscal measures to block the pressures towards urban dominance. And that will be done by reversing the trend towards concentration of economic power, both in town and country.

CHAPTER 11 FIXING THE TRUE VALUE OF LAND

The Finnish experience has already shown that a taxation system based on an accurate valuation of the productive capacity of each land holding, is both just and effective. It may be that, if farmers had the vision to adopt Henry George's original prescription, they could garner both moral credit to themselves and, finally, a system which gave them a rational world in which to function, together with a public which understood and correctly valued their activity. That prescription was the Land Value Tax.

George's idea - of which Einstein said "one cannot imagine a more beautiful combination of intellectual keenness, artistic form and fervent love of justice," - was that that portion of the value of any property which was not the product of the occupier's own labour or investment - its Economic Rent - should be payable as a tax to the community. Its elegance as a concept is breathtaking. Firstly, it has the virtue of being manifestly just, because it rests upon an objective assessment of the resources at the individual's disposal. Secondly, it is exceedingly easy to collect: tax avoidance would be virtually impossible. Land cannot be smuggled abroad, invested overseas, or hidden. Thirdly, it would prevent land from being kept idle in hope of speculative gain. At the same time, tax would only be levied on the true value of the asset in its current use. It would not tax enterprise, nor the additional income produced by good management or personal investment in buildings or material: so that everything the farmer put in by his own managerial skill or effort would receive its full and true reward.

Because it would inevitably lead to a more realistic assessment of the marginal revenue from increased production, it would remove the incentive to over-production and exploitation of the environment: the farmer would be able to choose his preferred level of production, and be taxed fairly on it, without the compulsion to run his land to its utmost in order to support heavy loans for its purchase in the first place. How existing loans would be taken care of is an interesting question: but it would seem just that the lender, who in most cases has the majority of the equity, should be required to carry the major part of the loss as land prices were forced down once the speculative element was eliminated from land occupancy. That may well be less damaging and painful than the likely effects of widespread bankruptcies of bank customers, as has happened in the USA - taking a number of banks with it. It may be less embarrassing, too, to the banks, to write down such a loss as a tax than as a write-off due to financial misjudgement.

Its benefits for conservation would not, however, stop there. Because such a tax would be levied impartially on all, towndwellers and countrypeople alike, it would put an end to much of the rivalry and resentment betwen the two. Certainly, it would have the merit of replacing the rating system by something manifestly more just, and which did not tax home improvements, or carry within it the temptation to vandalise or leave houses empty.

In the urban arena, its benefits would be almost incalculable. It would no longer be financially rewarding to keep sites of buildings empty for speculative reasons, forcing rents up through land shortage, and thereby reducing the opportunities for job creation. It would ensure that a larger part of company resources was available for the payment of employees, and that more profits remained available for productive investment. More importantly, that property investment became a far less seductive sink for company resources.

It would equalise the balance of return between office building and home building, giving back life to the inner cities: since the choice of use would also change the economic rent valuation: thus bringing back some sanity into land use, and stopping pure gain from being the dominating factor in development decisions - or rather, to allow social gain its proper weight. And it would release resources for the provision of public services on land which was no longer priced so high as to make their construction uneconomic or unjustifiable in accountancy terms.

More profound economic analyses of the effect of such a taxation strategy than can receive space in this book have been carried out. Amongst their conclusions are that a Land Value Tax introduced with full vigour and conviction could effectively produce the same fiscal yield as all existing taxes: and thus allow the abolition of income tax entirely; as well as greatly simplifying the whole collection of taxes, and reducing the amount of effort and staff it requires.

Such considerations are not fanciful: for modified versions of the tax have been used, with different degrees of beneficial effect, in the state of Victoria, Australia; in Japan, Taiwan and in Canada. In the early 19th century, before George first formulated his scheme, when Britain took over the island of Java from the Dutch, the governor installed, Sir Stamford Raffles, found an immensely complex array of taxes and restrictions on trade, imposed by the previous administration to sustain the Europeans' monopoly over Javanese trade. An account by the Australian A R Hutchinson gives a vivid picture of a somewhat familiar situation.

"There was a 15 per cent tax upon the production of rice, a poll-tax upon families, and market duties or tolls literally levied on every article produced by agriculture, manufacture or the petty arts. These somewhat resembled our Sales Tax and levies made by Egg Boards, Dried Fruits Boards and similar bodies. There was a tax upon the slaughter of buffaloes, which affected the price of food and restricted the breeding of animals. There was a charge upon the cost of transport of baggage and stores of every description and upon the feeding of travellers. There were obligations to render free labour service for public works and forced contribution to the government monopolies. Duties and charges on sea-borne commerce amounted to 46 per cent...

"Under the onslaught of these ferocious taxes whole districts became de-populated. There was a drift from the land to the towns and villages, and production of wealth was rapidly declining."

The picture may seem horribly familiar: for, as Hutchinson remarks, it is these same devices that are adopted by Europeans whrever they gain control. Call them import tarriffs to maintain threshold prices, Value-Added Tax etcetera, and the resemblance is complete.

Raffles's first action was to immerse himself in Javan history. He discovered that, under the traditional laws, landlordism did not exist, and there was no room for land speculation and land monopoly. Land might be held for use, provided the ground rent was paid over in full to the Government Authority. And that was the system he decided to reintroduce. He substituted a general tax on land value for all compulsory services, contingencies and forced deliveries, so that all farmers paid effectively a rent based on the productivity of the soil: fixed at two-fifths of the yield. And to make this an accurate measure, he instituted a complete cadastral survey to work out individual assessments. And indeed, activity and revenue did increase to a sufficient level to cover all normal costs of the government's operations.

This - over half a century before George first formulated his theory -was and still is the most complete implementation of Land Value taxation. Nowhere else, to date, has it been introduced fully: although urban land value taxation in South Korea, combined with the deliberate allotment and regulation of rural landholdings to crate a class of yeoman farmers, have both played a significant part in the South korean economic 'miracle'; and Hungary also implemented site value rating shortly after the First World War. The virtues claimed for it by Henry George - of reducing inflation in property values, stabilising the economy and re-directing investment to productive industry - have been significantly displayed even in the half-hearted trials it has been given.

Its virtue from the point of view of this book is that, for the first time, it would enable the use of land to be a genuine matter of choice. If it were to be wild, it would be because that was what society had chosen it to be: not merely the accident of neglect, lack of resources, or one man's greed.

CHAPTER 12 A CONFLICT OF MISUNDERSTANDINGS

"Your system is the problem that the world faces, not its solution. It is a system which maximises consumption in a world of limited resources, and which seeks to balance supply and demand only by restricting the number of high consumers to a very small proportion, about one-fifth, of the world's population. If China alone were to come into your system, and were to be rapidly successful within it - as we should be - we would break the system and bust the global economy. Think of a billion Chinese becoming two-car families, or consuming the amount of energy per head that an American or European family does and has done for years... it is impossible.

If the human race is to survive it is urgent that we all enter a system - but it will not be your system of high consumption, of mining the earth's resources as if there were no tomorrow, as if there were no children to live on into the next century. The system that must come will be harsh: it will seek to conserve rather than to consume; it will share more fairly according to need; it will seek for growth first among the poorest till their needs are met. It will not, as your system does, concentrate on increasing affluence as a prerequisite to decreasing poverty."

William Clark: Cataclysm

It is clear that the forces driving the development of the countryside in Britain have tended to have a negative effect. This is partly the result of our different circumstances, and partly the result of differences in the way the regulating factors have been applied: and these differences are themselves partly the product of national differences.

From the start, farm support measures have been applied in

a way calculated to increase property values, and to benefit the larger farmer more than the smaller. It has truly been a case of "to him that hath shall be given, and from him that hath not shall be taken even that which he hath". Even in the supposedly 'marginal' uplands, because hill farming supports have been paid per head of livestock, there has been a built-in incentive to increase farm size and increase stocking density, with a consequent destructive effect both on the upland environment and on the upland community. No attempt has been made to limit the size of enterprise or the number of stock eligible. A crude economic measure of "efficiency" has been applied which has in itself encouraged the conversion and "improvement" of moorland and upland grazing, and given greater financial muscle to the farmer who increased the size of his business.

This pretence that farming is a viable, self-sustaining activity which can be measured by purely business criteria, is the essence of the problem. The motives that lead people into farming are certainly not those which motivate ordinary business entrepreneurs. They are an amalgam of an independent drive to be one's own master, a liking for the land and the outdoor life, a wish for status and permanency, and other things. To dress them up in the respectable clothes of business is a falsification, or a gross oversimplification. And to run the financing and organisation of the countryside on that basis is dishonest. It is a system worthy of the days of the robber barons or when there was still a frontier to go beyond and take land: but it is absolutely unsuitable for an age when the country is very densely populated, colonisation is no longer possible, the scope for emigration is very limited and the pressures on land use intense.

It is hardly revolutionary, not even socialistic, to suggest that where large numbers of people are competing for a share of a limited asset, its distribution must needs be regulated. Unless some just and rational method of distribution and use-allocation is devised, there are bound to be consequences which are socially an environmentally harmful. To adopt a system wherein the prize goes to the strongest, and indeed the rules steadily strengthen his ability to take what he wants, all under claim of economic rationality, is perverse. I do not think that many farmers, who are essentially fair-minded people, and used to solving the problems of spreading resources over a number of competing needs, would disagree.

Yet there is little doubt that it is precisely as robber barons that they are perceived by some environmental campaigners. Book titles such as "The Theft of the Countryside", which utter appeals for more law and order, more planning controls in the regulation of land use, are manifestly cries for help from Robin Hood or some ideal policeman. Nor should they be unkindly mocked. While their prescriptions may be misconceived, the feeling which prompts their expression must be heeded and given its due value.

So how is countryside use best to be regulated? From the experience of the Soviet Union to that of Nyerere's Tanzania, it appears that central planning, or land nationalisation, is not an effective way. By the same token, the experience of the United States, with its current waves of farm bankruptcies, and its ability nationally to dominate and/or destabilise the entire world food market - and thereby cause tragic suffering in less-developed countries - the New Frontier or robber baron system is equally unaccceptable. Human experience, and the success of, for instance, Zimbabwe in feeding itself and generating a useful exportable surplus, as well as the third of all fruit and vegetable produce in the USSR which comes from private plots, indicate that the individual's ability to make something grow on a patch of land that he controls, is a fundamental and immensely productive power. At the same time, when that power becomes corrupted and confused with the accumulation of capital, the acquisition of status or political power, it becomes destructive.

Contrasting land-owning attitudes in France with those in Britain, there can be little doubt that the drive to accumulate land is itself a reflection of our continuing clearly-defined class system and the hunger for status that it engenders. The fact that the status of property owning is today open to a wider section of the population does not change that fundamental, ignoble instinct: indeed in many towns - where the willingness to move home as soon as there is a profit to be made by trading up is evidenced by estate agents' boards in every street - it has contributed to the destabilisation of society, the denial of roots to growing children, familiar neighbourhoods and relationships to the home-based adult, marital strain, and the extension of cash valuation to areas more properly valued on moral, psychological, social or community bases. "Home" and "property" become confused, and by the same process "security" becomes interchangeable with "wealth", "love" with "money", and the whole quality of life becomes degraded. "Price" and "value", "good" and "goods" become indistinguishable, possessions become power, and human relations become based upon purchase and control, rather than sharing and spontaneity. A prison from which there is no escape.

Further, as in all societies where the distribution of resources is governed by might, wealth or opportunism, the finite nature of their supply is often lost sight of in the scramble to get one's share, or more. The simple economic law that our agriculture, on a less-than-ideal base of climate and geology, is only able to be as productive as it is by monopolising more than its share of world resources, is scarcely understood, even by those directly engaged in farm production. The fact that the ability to consume or accommodate production is itself a resource of strictly limited size, is hardly perceived: and anyone who voices the fact that over-consumption and over-production are both gross and ugly forms of greed heedless of the human needs of others, is dismissed as extremist or eccentric.

Yet our arrogant appropriation of the right to produce and market is demonstrably exercised with very great violence. For instance: the proceeds of selling food received under aid programmes makes up over 10 per cent of the revenue of the Bangla Desh government. The loss of that aid would have a catastrophically destabilising effect on that country's economy. But the threat of its withdrawal was used recently to induce the government to abandon its plans to prohibit the marketing of drugs and pesticides banned in their countries of origin - which happened also to be the aid donors. Again, the withholding of cheap food supplies from the Allende government in Chile denied it the economic leeway it needed to cushion political discontent among the urban middle class while it went about necessarily costly social and land reforms.

By the same token, the British farmer who expands his farm, buys a larger tractor and sacks one of his men, sells off the cottage that man's family used to occupy to a car-borne commuter or weekender who shops in town, thus allowing the primary school roll, trade in the village shop and local bus usage to sink below the level of viability, is taking unto himself more than his share of resources, at the expense of the community at large. And talking about his hard work, business efficiency and his contribution to import-saving or exports, is merely a diversion. His gain is at the expense of the social bankruptcy of the rural area.

All of which is not to say that farming should be restricted or abolished in favour of imports from the world market. It is, however, to say very clearly that the organisation of the countryside needs to be based on a clear assessment both of the true resources available, and of a people-based economy rather than accountants' measurements of success. If everyone were allowed to open a barber's shop in his or her front room, there would not be enough hair needing cutting to go around: yet, when it comes to growing wheat, that is exactly what we allow. In some sectors, such as potatoes, sugar and milk, controls have been imposed: so that the suggestion that they may be necessary will not strike people as unreasonable. But the way in which the limits have been calculated is still eccentric in the extreme. Sugar quotas have been fixed in a way which effectively destroys the market for the cane sugar which is the only crop of several countries in the tropics; and the market has been protected in a way which destroys their genuine climatic advantage which allows year-round production at an efficiency of which our farmers could only dream. Potatoes, since their transport involves the shifting of a considerable quantity of water, and since they are basically a temperate crop, are more logical to produce; and output regulation is only necessary to prevent the wilder swings of the market. Milk is a natural farm product in a temperate, grass-growing climate, and has a vital structural role to play in the rural economy because it is the only farm enterprise that produces a regular monthly income on which the smaller farmer, who cannot afford to borrow and wait a whole season for his returns, can live. But the increase of milk production to levels far above any that can realistically be needed or consumed, is a self-evident nonsense.

The reason why the surpluses have accumulated is that we have refused to consider any raison d'tre for the farm population other than food production, and considered it better for them to be producing food that no one needs, because that is "real farming", than do other things which are really wanted, such as maintaining the countryside. It has to be said, and loudly, that producing food no one wants is not real farming at all: it is playing. And to sugggest that if farmers are stopped from such play, the countryside will no longer be kept looking the way we want it, is outrageous nonsense. If keeping it looking that way is what we want, then let us work out how to keep it so, and pay the cost.

Indeed, it is the matter of cost which lies at the heart of things. If the true cost of any given countryside use were clear to those who make it and to those who consume it, decisions of what land should be given to which use would become far more straightforward to make. And the best way of achieving this clarity is to establish the economic rent - the opportunity cost - of every piece of land.

Again, this suggestion is neither so fanciful, nor so cumbersome, as might be suggested. The re-rating of agricultural land has been suggested in many quarters. It has now become part of the Labour party's election manifesto, although more for doctrinaire reasons of attacking a popular scapegoat than because the questions of land use and valuation have been thought through at all thoroughly. If the revenue so raised is administered by an urban-based bureaucracy, it will simply accelerate the development of the towns' colonial relationship with the countryside. If, on the other hand, it is part of an even-handed assessment of resource and contribution across the whole community, urban and rural, it could be the beginnings of a new social and economic dispensation. At present, job creation in small communities is often blocked because of the cost of providing infrastructure - roads, water, sewers and so on - because such spending is usually concentrated on towns. A system where both revenue and need for services were acknowledged as arising equally in rural areas, could give a new dynamism to the whole economy.

The valuation of land would not be an impossible task, and would lay the ground for an honest and visibly just system. Complete cadastral surveys have been already made in other countries, are regularly updated and used as the basis of their taxation systems. In this country, the Institute of Terrestrial Ecology's kilometre-square classification of land use and quality already provides the basis of such a survey; and it would not be impossible to upgrade that to an accurate assessment of economic rent. What William the Conqueror's men were able to do in the space of a couple of years on horseback for Domesday, let no one say could not be done in these days of accurate geological mapping, soil survey, motor cars, aerial photography, MAFF statistics and computers.

Once done, it would provide a clear and reasonable indication of the value of the land occupied by each farmer: and a basis for taxation far more just and simple than any we have at present. Where the land was manifestly insufficient to support a family, or it was desired to keep that land occupied or farmed in a particular, sub-economic manner in order to maintain its present condition and appearance, a negative tax or occupational subsidy would have to be allowed. None of this is unreasonable, nor need it be regarded as dishonourable or demeaning to the farmer. All farming is at present subsidised; much would not be viable on a strict economic analysis: and if a particular style of countryside or rural community is a good desired by the majority of the population, then let the farmer produce that good and be fairly paid for it. (As I write, the French government has obviously recognised that fact, and is paying out 2.5billion Francs survival subsidy to its farmers after the disastrous year of 1986.)

At the same time, let the farmer who occupies a large area of high quality land, produces a large crop and derives a substantial income from it, pay tax proportional to the advantage he enjoys. That which is produced by his own labour and capital in the form of machinery and other inputs, is justly his; but the economic value of the land is not. It is this confusion of the market price of land with capital that has bedevilled the whole economics of farming and conservation. At present, if a farmer is induced by a management agreement

137

not to carry out some farming operation which damages the countryside, he is entitled, under the Wildlife and Countryside Act, not only to compensation for the loss of income from the production foregone, but also to the loss of capital value in the land, That was not morally his in the first place.

Perhaps the justice of this idea may be more easily seen if applied to the urban situation. Here, the man who has title to a piece of land in the centre of town has an advantage not available to him who only has a piece further out. Because of the action of the community in creating the town, its roadways, its public transport, car parks, drains and services, that land can be used for building offices or shops, being at the centre of trade and interchange. Under the present system, that fortuitous advantage derived from from the growth, activity and investment of the community as a whole becomes consolidated into the capital value of the individual owner's land. In the same way, the subsidies and improvement grants given to farmers to stabilise the market and increase our national food security have become capitalised in private land values. And these mean that anyone wanting to acquire the use of land for farming purposes has had to take on heavy loan burdens which impose a fixed cost on the farm enterprise which is entirely irrelevant and distorting to the farm business - and reinforces the need for price support in order to keep it able to service its debts. Until farming is unhitched from the capital value of land, it will never be possible to work out a rational system of land use, or establish what activities really need support, and how much of it.

CHAPTER 13 AVOIDING RURAL SOCIAL BANKRUPTCY

My telly eats people
especially on the news.

Little people   My telly
with no shoes   eats people
Little people   if you don't
with no food   believe me
Little people   look inside
crying   the belly
Little people   of my telly.
dying

John Agard: I Din Do Nuttin

It is comparatively easy to sit at a word processor elaborating theories of how to reconstruct the world. However, I believe this book has highlighted a number of forces and problems, with both a national and an international dimension, which will have to be confronted before real progress can be made towards protecting the environment and satisying human need. It is already abundantly clear that, if they are not so tackled, the prospects for the human race and for the global environment are dismal. It may be helpful to recap the forces at work.

Firstly, there is the world-wide trend towards urbanisation. Partly the product of population growth, it is accelerated and exacerbated by a second trend towards concentration of economic power: which expresses itself very clearly in the control of land.

Domestically, these forces display themselves on both the rural and urban scenes; and the two intermesh far more than is widely realised. The ongoing movement towards farm amalgamation, producing larger and larger farms - which has long since passed the point where real economies of scale apply - is reinforced by the action of the Common Agricultural Policy, which brings greater benefits and rewards to larger farmers. In all cases, those paying higher marginal rates of tax benefit more than those who are merely making a living, either on the land or off it. Under the present system, mere downward pressure on product prices is likely to produce a landscape made up of large-scale arable farms and intensive livestock units interspersed with Sites of Special Scientific or Scenic Interest. As was said in Chapter 3, the pressure towards intensification is shown by the fact that the UK dairy industry, in the eight years from 1976, increased its output by 20 per cent even as the real price of milk dropped by the same percentage. In the same period, the cereal price went down by 26 per cent, but output doubled.

Where intensive production is possible, it will continue; while poorer land less responsive to inputs will be less well-farmed. In fact, 'lower inputs' could mean careless farming - using wide-spectrum chemicals rather than more expensive selective ones; skimping on maintenance and machinery cost so that more of the sprays go adrift; sub-standard, poorly-maintained buildings: adding up to an only partly-farmed countryside and an increasingly derelict landscape.

In the residential market - both urban and rural - once again those who possess capital, particularly land-based capital (and this includes home ownership) have a marked economic advantage over those who do not: and that advantage is continually increased by the ratchet of inflation in property values which, in the south-east, is proceeding at nearly ten times the rate of the increase in the basic cost of living. As pointed out by the Duke of Edinburgh's Committee on Housing Policy, mortgage tax relief provides a far greater subsidy to home owners than is available to occupants of housing rented in the public sector.

In both spheres, the mechanism works unswervingly towards the fixing and reinforcing of privilege: and thus to promote an attitude of "Pull up the ladder, Jack: I'm all right." Those who are just hanging on to the bottom of the ladder are in considerable danger of being shaken off in the process.

On a world scale, the same situation is to be seen. The prosperity and living security of the industrialised nations was founded, and still depends on, their appropriating far more than their share of the world's resources and living space. The United States, with roughly 5 per cent of the world's population, consumes some 30 per cent of the world's resources; and the nations of Western Europe are not far behind. Our industries are built on the appropriation and jealously-guarded control of their markets, which have been built into dependence. While we have widely refused to open our markets to the products of their infant industries - indeed at the 1986 round of GATT talks, the USA has taken further steps to exclude finished cloths woven in developing countries from locally-produced natural fibres - we have used every means possible to encourage them to buy the output of ours: including the encouragement to borrow from our banks to finance purchases on a grand scale of equipment and infrastructure often not appropriate or even maintainable in their situation. The analogy of the unlettered British consumer being enticed into opening a department store 'budget account' to buy a sophisticated knitting machine or computer that he will never learn how to work, in the belief that it will not only finance the account payments but solve all his other financial problems, and then being sunk by the debt, is apt and accurate.

The twin arm of this mechanism is our jealously-guarded control of world markets in commodities - of which food is only a part. Shamefully, we shall always be able to outbid the poor as buyers in the world food market, and always able to beat them down as sellers. The strength of our agricultural system IS a weapon of political and economic dominance.

As former World Bank Vice President William Clark says in "Cataclysm", his fictionalised forecast of a world economic crisis, "Why should governments and people in the South go on paying billions to the rich North as rent on money long since used up to buy goods in markets dominated by the rich; markets whose great magic seemed to be to inflate the price demanded for Northern goods and deflate the price paid for Southern commodities?"

On the agricultural front, our surplus production is NOT due to the inherent superiority of our farming. To a far greater extent, it is the product of just the same process of appropriating a larger-than-fair share of the world's resources - often to finance developments which actually increase, not decrease production costs. Although inherent stable, neither our climate nor our soils are better for farm production to the degree that our output exceeds that of developing countries: it is more that we are richer, can buy more fertilisers, more machinery, more animal feed components, and push them through the more luxurious farming machine we have acquired for ourselves. The driver of a Rolls Royce is not necessarily a better driver than that of a Citron 2cv: all that is certain is that he is more comfortable, takes up much more road space, and consumes a great deal more fuel. His manners and consideration for other road users may actually be far worse.

The effects of our bloated, privileged agriculture can also be seen in the environment, both physical and social. The concentration of the right to produce in the hands of a dwindling number of farmers has contributed to a withering of the rural community: as the land-based workforce has been decimated by advances in 'productivity' - which have concentrated the profit in the hands of those fewer farmers - so the village shops, schools and bus services which existed to serve it have shrivelled and been closed. In some parishes now, the resident farmer has become extinct.

But the concentration of industry and retailing have been the main motors of the process, in which farmers have been carried along as junior partners. The resulting large farms supply the mass-buying agencies of the big supermarkets on the edges of towns to which the former customers of the village shops now go. At the same time, the farmers profit from the inflation of rural property values by selling off cottages no longer needed for farm workers, to urban out-movers, who retain their urban shopping and social habits, but ally themselves with the big farmer in resisting any business or industrial development in the rural areas which would for him push up farm labour wages, and for them depress speculative gains in property values.

In just the same way we, the former colonists who seized the best land in the developing countries, have now passed it on, but tied it up in contracts to supply raw materials to our multinational industries: and at the same time take powerful measures to prevent the development of local industry which could add value to those materials and impinge on the security of our markets.

The mechanisms are the same, at whatever level we examine the situation: and so are the motives. Domestically, in Britain, their crudity and ugliness are well-disguised in an urbane and civilised wrapping of manners: privilege dressing itself as stewardship, acquisitiveness as successful enterprise, small charity and patronage as social concern. By the same token, internationally, so-called development aid provided only to finance purchases of high-tech products which give trade to our industries but often destroy existing communities, undermine their agriculture and ensure that the poor pass from subsistence to irremediable poverty, are presented as generosity; and contributions to charitable development agencies are all that salves our consciences with its tiny tithe of atonement. Our sufficiency is the twin, the other face of the coin of their incapacity.

What we are discussing is no less than the proper sharing and use of the world's resources between a population whose size already means there is not much to spare. Nor is it anything but hypocrisy for us to blame that growth on the self-indulgence or over-breeding of other nations. Our own populations tripled in barely a century, and doubled again in a further half-century, not so long ago; and we seized by brute force the resources to bring them to the standard of living where population growth naturally slows down. Where insecurity is the norm, and manual labour the only resource available to provide the means of life, it is natural that people will have more children - if only so that enough survive to gather firewood, scratch the soil, tend the animals and look after their parents in old age. Similarly, knowing we can buy feed for our stock, and having guaranteed markets for their produce, we can well afford to select, breed and manage their numbers. In a situation where grazing will depend on the vagaries of weather, plant supply, and competition for resources, stock numbers are the readiest index of wealth; and it is natural for them to be multiplied as long as resources exist to support them, and for them to starve when those resources fail.

So what are the remedies? We have already reached the stage where resources must be more equitably distributed to allow mere survival to all. In a world where 15 million children die each year from the direct or indirect consequences of malnutrition, that fact cannot be ignored. And to export our surplus cow's milk in the form of baby formula to Africans who may not have the means readily to sterilise bottles and mixture, knowing that it will be inferior in health terms to breast milk, and will cost a third of their monthly income to buy a supply for one two-month infant, cannot respectably be called a nutritional solution. Rather, a corrosive one dissolving the very substance of their domestic economy.

The first step must be to arrive at a sensible inventory, not of product, but of productive resources: for it is access to those which offers the only long-term possibility of human dignity and self-support. In the less-developed countries, it is access to land and control of productive resources by small farmers, which spells the difference between a healthy agriculture and starvation. In countries with year-round sunshine to support plant growth, the involvement of peasant farmers in the production of crops for export gives them a chance of income which then feeds into and lifts the whole economy. Growing manioc for the European animal feed industry fitted well into the regime of small farmers in northern Thailand because it is a reliable, disease-free crop with good drought resistance for the dry season: and vegetables for their own sustenance could be fitted in between manioc crops during the rainy season. However, even there, this hungry crop rapidly exhausted soils the small farmer could not afford to replenish with fertiliser; and the cassava cash crop is now substantially in the hands of larger farmers with capital in the southern lowlands. Growing cash crops for export needs to be carefully introduced, not imposed as a budgetary panacea. Possibly, oil palm is capable of integration into a mixed-cropping agroforestry system to provide a genuine increase of economic level without impoverishment of the individual producer. But when land is gathered into large holdings for commercial, highly-mechanised exploitation, little employment is generated for the population at large, and the profit stays in the hands of the large landowners, benefiting the national economy very little.

The remedy, there as here, is basically to strengthen the position of the small producer. This not only achieves greater justice and a sufficiency for a greater number of people: it also produces a fundamentally more stable situation, injects more vigour into, and cycles more resources through, the rural economy. If we brought the level of employment in agriculture in this country even back up to the average level of our European partners, unemployment would be reduced by 1 million, and the quality of life for some 5 million children, women and men would be vastly improved. At present, what was largely a craft industry has been transformed into a highly intensive, technology-based one with all the characteristics of large industry: pollution, concentration of production and dependence on non-renewable resources. Countries like Japan, France and Germany have their industrial sectors under-pinned by a ground of small-scale farmers. This provides both a more resilient and a more stable economy. Also, it has to be said, a more economical and environment-sensitive agriculture. Using integrated pest management taking advantage of natural predators, making better use of straw and animal manures, conserving grass with less waste - has a greater labour need.

Nor is this to say that the massive capital investment that has been made in agriculture in this country in the last 30 years or so can or should be thrown away. Small-scale farming needs to be brought back into healthy equality with large, not to replace it. The unavoidable fixed cost investment of around £200 per hectare of cereal land, cannot be legislated out of existence; and it would be folly to try to reduce relatively inexpensive inputs which will protect and improve the growing crop. Similarly, each dairy cow entrains a fixed cost of close on £300 which has to be covered, whatever the yield level. Reducing cow numbers while maintaining yield levels, and producing as much feed as possible at home, is likely to be the best course in the dairy industry. In cereal production, it has been estimated, doubling the cost of Nitrogen would induce a mere 10 per cent cut in its use and about a 2 per cent drop in yield. Farm N quotas would still be open to switching fertiliser from grass - which receives the major part of it at present - to cereals. Land will not be voluntarily 'set aside' unless farmers are sure that it will not thereby be excluded from any future hectarage quota. The most promising strategies are probably strengthening incentives to work field corners and margins less intensively; and perhaps an easily-policeable ban on planting cereals before October -which would automatically reduce intensity,and exclude some of the heavier, more marginal soils. This kind of approach has the virtue of not requiring any overt revolution or political upheaval, and being easily monitored. In the longer run, cereals may well be the best renewable energy source: and farm-scale plants to convert them to bio-oil for onward sale to industry the farmer's best way of adding value to his crop at the farm gate.

Happily, technical improvements in the pipeline mostly appear scale-neutral: that is, they will bring benefit to the small farmer in the same proportion as the large, without demanding heavy capital investment. Biological control of weeds, diseases and pests to replace chemical sprays are in fairly immediate prospect, perhaps by 1990. Breeding advance promises crops with improved stress resistance (especially to drought) by the same date; better tolerance of weed competition and greater efficiency of nitrogen use by 1995. Genetic engineering should deliver cereals with the legume's capacity to fix nitrogen through microbial root nodules by the year 2000, with insect resistance following five years later. All these will reduce the number and quantity of purchased inputs, strengthening the hand, while reducing the costs of, the family farm.

To increase numbers of smaller farmers, a measure of land reform could be achieved simply by the measures suggested in the Minority Report of the Northcliffe Committee: namely, of placing a limit on the amount of land that may be beneficially occupied (2,000 acres was the reasonable suggestion) and by limiting tax reliefs to those whose main income is derived from farming. Effectively, this would be a gentle introduction of a

Land Quota system. In the Court of public opinion, it is difficult to see there being any significant political opposition to this manifestly just and necessary measure, once the issues were properly explained. Certainly, there is a strong case for levying Capital Transfer Tax or its equivalent on any land held simply as an investment or a tax-losing sideline, and any above a size of holding agreed to be sufficient for economic management. Land is not just another form of capital, it is a basic resource, and all our European partners place some control on its occupancy.

Nor is agriculture just another industry, to be exposed to the untempered forces of economics. The vagaries of weather introduce a degree of uncertainty and variability which make market stabilisation measures indispensible. It is likely that farmers who have geared up to large-scale production will continue and be well able to survive without heavy protection, and still make profits at world market prices: but the adoption of threshold pricing, whereby the first unit of production receives a price supported at a sufficient level to guarantee a living to the smaller producer, is obviously desirable - and in the line of current EEC thinking on co-responsibility levy exemptions. Such a policy would in due course tend to lead to the subdivision of over-large farms, opening the way to new entrants who could improve the vigour and quality of British farming; the diversification of production on farms (producing a more mixed agriculture, which is environmentally desirable); a reduction in output and therefore in unnecessary inputs; and would encourage large-scale farmers to search for new types of non-surplus production, for instance timber.

To operate such a system, it would be essential for land ownership to be clearly established in all cases, if only to prevent phoney subdivisions of holdings under the same effective ownership. It is perhaps hardly surprising, when so much privilege, wealth and social power depend on it, that the ownership of land in this country is still so disguised that it is impossible to establish clearly its details: but there can be no rational excuse for continuing to tolerate such a situation. A proper land register, with clear details of who owns what and profits from it, is indispensible for any clear analysis of the allocation and use of resources.

As a first step towards this, a proper survey of land quality, climate and use needs to be drawn up. Without it, all use and development depends on whim, personal interest, and ability to corner supplies of capital, assistance and resources. Once the quality and productive potential of each piece of land is known, we at last have a rational basis on which to decide, finance or tax its use. I believe that many farmers would actually welcome such an objective categorisation of land value, because it would take away the argument about the true value of their holdings; and prevent a great deal of ignorant envy. I think the more intelligent and fair-minded ones would even welcome a manifestly fair and just basis for taxation, compensation or support for their activity, too.

Such a complete cadastral survey is already maintained in both Sweden and Finland: where forest holdings are actually taxed on their agreed potential yield. There is no reason why such a system, embracing ADAS and some of the functions of the Department of the Environment, the conservation agencies and the Inland Revenue, should not arrive at a genuinely agriculture-sensitive and landscape-enhancing management of the British countryside.

To prevent land speculation is, once the will to do so exists, wonderfully simple. Taxing the gains from speculation is, and has been demonstrated to be, completely useless: in fact, it merely encourages hoarding in expectation of the removal of the measure intended to prevent it. The application of an annual tax on the full economic rental value of land is all that is required. Thereby, the owner is obliged to keep the land in productive use to fund the tax; and any speculative increase in value is immediately returned to the community - since such increase is certainly produced by the community's own action and expenditure. On farmland, letting thereby becomes as ready a way of paying the tax as farming it in hand: thus re-opening the farming ladder to new entrants. The provision of central services on let estates could provide increased properly-earned income to the landowner, while combining the economies of scale with the efficiency of family farming.

Only when this has been done can sensible plans be made for the actual use of land. Clearly, where population is high enough to leave little spare in the way of resources, their allocation needs to be increasingly consciously decided and regulated. It is entirely proper to decide that given areas of the country are indispensible for recreation, spiritual or physical; that others are essential as nature reserves or wildlife or landscape banks. Where such use is selected, and dictates a lower level of exploitation than is necessary to support the local population, the land value has to become negatively-taxed: that is, society has to decide to allocate a portion of its resources to finance that supply for itself. But since the national survey has already determined the productive economic value of that particular portion of land, the relative cost of that supply to society can be accurately related to the land's value; the income due to its occupant for maintaining a given level of grazing, hedge maintenance and so on honourably determined and paid without patronage. Where forest planting is desired, for instance, as in Scandinavia, a complete tax holiday would be granted for the 20 or 25 years until the plantation began to produce an income; together with grants towards the cost of establishment as already paid - which are the community's contribution towards the cost of creating a national asset. The waiving or negativing of the tax thus becomes a clear financial signal of approval of a given use - which can be argued, justified and agreed in advance of investment.

Further, because the ability to exploit and gather unfair gains is restrained, the need for envy or resentment, and the competition to seize such resources and protect them from others, is removed. This is not socialism, nor land nationalisation: it is actually permitting the market correctly to determine resource values, and to participate in the process of regulating their use.

At the same time, because it is land value that is taxed, and neither the user's labour nor improvements carried out on it by the individual occupant, nor the home or business he constructs upon it, the proper pride and investment in provision and accommodation for one's family are not subject to any penalty or disincentive; although the cumulative improvement to a neighbourhood which is the sum of all such efforts accrues in due course to the community as a whole rather than the individual home purchaser, as land tax values gradually increase. But because there is no incentive to individual speculation, it becomes far easier to make rational decisions on land use.

All of this has to be established on a basis of respect, consultation with and involvement of, the farming and rural community, not attack, dismissal or pushing it around. It is a very major mental step for farmers to relinquish the comforting but delusory belief that they are entrepreneurs running their own businesses in a real market, and accept the idea of doing what is in the public interest - although that was the stated purpose of the 1947 Agriculture Act. The more so since the public interest has now changed. In 1947, it actually required them to maximise food production, which went along nicely with the entrepreneurial delusion. Today, food surpluses, the world economic situation and the mounting crisis of the environment precipitated by the business/industrial approach, demand that thinking be re-educated. (It should be remembered, however, that it is only because we enjoy unprecedented food security that we are in a position to pay attention to conservation.)

It is necessary that farmers start to discuss openly what they do and why they do it: and it is equally necessary that the general public and the authorities take the trouble to inform themselves of the actual physical constraints under which farmers work. Realistic research needs to be made into the possibilities of farming with lower inputs, and into enhancing the viability of the smaller, family-sized farm. Demonstrations of practical, successful, sensitive farming need to be more common and open to visit and inspection, so that the idea of planting trees to enhance landscape value, farming at less than maximum intensity to strengthen other than mere business features of the farm, become part of the farmers' mental furniture. When that is done, they will be able to enter into discussion and tackle the devising of more environment-sensitive working systems with the same sense of mental challenge and reward as they have derived from business farming. It is necessary that they should learn to identify their own interests with the public interest under the new dispensation. Looking after wildlife and enhancing the landscape are not just an investment for the nation: they also add in many cases to the earning power of the land shown at present, by the addition of some £480 per hectare (£200/acre) to its capital value.

The management agreements concluded with farmers by National Parks officers to safeguard important scenic or ecological features have already achieved an admirable balance of firmness, sensitivity and expert understanding of the personal and technical needs of the farm livelihood. They provide a far better model for deciding levels of activity than the present division between the Countryside Commission and the Nature Conservancy, which, according to one recent major study, has often precipitated conflict, and produced "an effete and denatured notion of landscape and a remote and elitist notion of nature" (another example of the ineffectiveness of urban-based attempts to regulate or administer the countryside?). Above all, such regulation should not be bureaucratic or legalistic, but firmly based in an understanding of the working of the countryside, its economic and community life. This can include the involvement of ADAS or some organisation with the confidence of farmers in a balanced discussion which will safeguard the countryside in a way which is seen as technically realistic by those who have to implement it, at the same time as preventing speculation or exploitation.

A good example of such an organisation, not tainted with the single-minded drive for large production, but still respected by farmers as having its feet firmly planted in the soil of practical farming, is the Farming and Wildlife Advisory Group. This has, tapping both public and government funds, begun to build up a country-side network of groups which combine people with a proper professional training in agriculture with expert conservationists and help work out together with farmers an appropriate dynamic balance between farming and the natural world. This is quite different from mere preservation, and a great deal healthier.

The same approach needs to be adopted towards the reinvigoration of rural social and economic life. The development of suitable business and light industry in rural communities - which can provide flexible employment for mothers with school-age children, part-time work for those who also have family or community responsibilities, readily-available employment without long-distance commuting, and locally-generated wealth and demand to feed into the community and its services - becomes rational and desirable. Encouragement needs to be given, both through allocation and distribution of resources, and also by deliberate selective relaxation of planning controls, to reverse the decline of the rural community. At present, "the countryside" in many mouths, is a synonym for a flight from industry, which is perceived as risky, frightening and dirty. Nonsense decisions result: like the case of the farrier refused permission to re-open the old smithy in a Wiltshire village - which had a quite sufficient horse population to give him a living, together with some ancillary work like gate-making - "in case he became too successful and wanted to expand".

The Council for Small Industries in Rural Areas (COSIRA) now forecasts 1 in 10 of city dwellers moving out into the country during the next 30 to 40 years - that is, close on 5 million people by 2025 - and favours gradual expansion of towns and villages rather than a new garden city programme. "Most large villages of around 1,500 population could have a small industrial area with a dozen firms providing about 100 jobs. Smaller villages could take three or four businesses either in purpose-bulit premises, or converted schools, chapels, railway stations and farm buildings. The downward trend in rural population has already, in some southern counties, stopped, and taken an upward turn. The need is to give this new population a raison d'tre and activities which will involve it in the rural community as participant and contributor, not a resented and impeding appendage.

Friends of the Earth came out at the 1986 Nottingham town planning summer school in favour of a rural resettlement programme together with moves to bring rural occupations into cities. Positive discrimination in favour of locally-based enterprise, locally-employed population, and local profit and activity-generation, should be exercised against the national and multinational operators. If this is done, true conservation which arises from productive and caring use of the land, rather than its mere exploitation, will prosper; and community pride will achieve far more than sterile legislation from above. Life will take the place of an embalmed suspended animation.

The re-creation of a vigorous, self-supporting, multi-faceted rural society becomes possible once again: and within that, farm-based enterprises have a real part to play. The new business may often be one which adds value to agricultural produce; or helps to market the special qualities and advantages of the rural situation. There is no reason why, in areas where scenery is attractive but agricultural productivity low, the building of holiday homes or log cabins or, eventually, homes to retire to, should not be encouraged, within proper planning and husbanding of the total landscape resources. The Scandinavians manage to provide such a home for a large proportion of families: buying the land in their 20s, building the cabin in their 30s, improving it in their 40s and finally retiring to it, even in their national parks and nature reserves; and generate thereby a considerable additional input to their total economy in building materials, food, boats to run on lakes, plus services supplied by rural food shops, garages and so on - which helps strengthen the links of experience and understanding between town and country. Britain's case is particular, since it is now effectively a completely urbanised country: even our agriculture is fundamentally industrialised, and the distinction between town and country is no longer relevant or adequate as a basis for planning. A new outlook seeing society as a whole is required.

Extending the analogy to the international scene, calls for a greater degree both of goodwill and decision. However, it appears that people at large may be coming to the point where they can appreciate, and willingly embrace the need for it. The popular desire to redistribute resources and remedy deprivation expressed by the doubling of relief agencies' income in the past year, and such events as Live Aid and Sport Aid gives grounds to hope society at large may be capable of making the imaginative leap from personal acquisitiveness back to communal responsibility and inter-dependence. It is clearly insane and unjustifiable for us to consume resources producing some agricultural commodities which can be more economically produced elsewhere in the world, and in the process give otherwise irreplaceable sustenance to other, weaker economies. Sugar is perhaps the most glaring example of such a commodity; but the commandeering of poorer farmers' markets to dispose of our surpluses at less reward to ourselves than we are depriving them of, is equally illogical. At the same time, the market imperative at present usually prevents us from using our super-self-sufficiency to support and satisfy growing demand in countries that are investing their resources in development, and thus cushion them against the inevitable social friction the growth process generates: which would be entirely desirable.

And while it is not, perhaps, open to us to dictate the organisation of other societies, the withholding of support or connivance from economic organisation which reinforces impoverishment and the concentration of privilege, is proper, and to be encouraged. Per contra, the encouragement - whether for the benefit of repayment to our banks, or the supply of our industries - of the concentration of the best land into cash crop growing for export purely for the profit of a small elite of landowners is to aid and abet the very forces which throw up the evils we most deplore.

In the last analysis, we are only at the beginning of a process, which will return us to a condition much nearer the beginnings of human occupancy of this earth. It starts with the realisation that no man or country is an island entire of itself: but that the sea which surrounds us all is the same. And the water is rising, rapidly.

CHAPTER 14 TURNING BACK TOWARDS LIFE

Oh rose, thou art sick.
The invisible worm That flies in the night,
In the howling storm,

Hath found out thy bed Of crimson joy:
And his dark secret love Does thy life destroy.

           William Blake: The Sick Rose

The human population, when not interrupted by famine, war or pestilence, tends to increase geometrically. But the impact of mankind on the environment appears to increase at an even steeper rate, so that a doubling of numbers may quadruple or quintuple the degree of environmental damage. This is because both the products and demands of larger groups of human beings tend to be greater than those of individual families or small groups, and therefore more consuming and more polluting.

As population mounts, social and economic organisation becomes more complex and sophisticated. And this produces the second great engine of destruction: urbanisation. For the poorer majority of its inhabitants, driven or drawn off the land they formerly occupied as peasants, the city is a great distilling-vat of misery; but it and its ramifying control of the whole economy is also a prime creator of that misery.

Everyone is aware of the degradation of the world environment, but most people's awareness does not go far beyond the symptoms. Causes are still very poorly understood and disasters elsewhere may be simplistically attributed to drought, farming methods or population pressure, with no understanding of the overall system which harnesses these factors into a team and makes them work together so that the total effect is greater than the sum of its parts.

Simply treating symptoms by imposing controls, creating nature reserves, or flying loads of grain to famine areas or prescribing birth control or building dams for irrigation and electricity generation tend at best to be palliatives and often in the long run to make things worse. Like doctors, we may suppress one symptom only to see others break out in the same place or elsewhere. The world's sickness is multi-factorial, and demands a co-ordinated and compatible range of remedies.

What makes it easy for us to ignore this is the fact that we happen to live in a highly-privileged, environmentally well-buffered and comparatively wealthy part of the world which has long since reached the level of economic and industrial development necessary for self-sustaining comfort. Because, compared to the Ethiopians or the landless peasants of Bangla Desh or north-east Brazil, we enjoy a beautiful countryside and our general level of wealth is above the crisis level, we are able to overlook the fact that the same structure, the same infection, and the same forces have long been at work in our country. Our environmental concerns, while sometimes dramatically presented by campaigners or the media, are perceived as being matters of adjustment, decoration; easily achieved with a little determination and effort, or discipline of a small sector.

In other parts of the world, the chief weakening factor is poverty, It is poverty, not overpopulation or the vagaries of climate, which causes famine. There is more than enough food to satisfy world demand, but a large part of that demand is not effective because it doesn't have the money to satisfy its needs. That poverty is produced by a process of concentration of power and possession of land in the hands of a small proportion of the population. Their exploitation of it inevitably dispossesses and disadvantages others - the majority - and leads to environmental degradation.

What is even less appreciated is that we, the wealthy minority of the world's population, also profit from that process. We are the exploiting elite of the world population.

Our activities and our interests, which we firmly and carefully defend, tend to encourage and exacerbate the process which impoverishes the majority of other populations, and as their poor majority struggle to survive, denuding the environment in the process, we become passive accomplices in the destruction.

Every cheap cotton garment we buy is made at the price of some loss of fertility in the soil on which the hungry cotton crop grows. A bargain pack of Dutch bacon in a supermarket has been cheaply grown on energy sucked from the soils of peasant farms in Thailand, soya from land which formerly supported peasants in Brazil, peanuts bought cheaply from West Africans sacrificing their land to buy our technologies and high-priced energy. Our tea still costs a penny a cup because made with the sweat of underprivileged pickers.

But the forces and the powers which produce this extreme impoverishment elsewhere are also at work in our more cushioned society. The same concentration of land ownership into comparatively few hands, the same sacrifice of land to the industrial or financial interests of a small sector, take place here as throughout the market economies. Over half the land in this country still belongs to 1 per cent of the population, and the 6 per cent who own nearly 85 per cent of it occupy virtually all the positions of political power, as well as all the seats on the boards of large companies and institutions. And while they may choose, for reasons of amenity, to have country seats, the levers and the interlinking mechanisms by which they exercise control are all part of the urban-based centralisation of power.

It is an urbane exercise of power, motivated less by greed, manipulation or malignity than an unshakeable historic conviction of the right to manage. And that means manage according to business, as opposed to moral, social or environmental principles.

Under this management, the whole thrust of agricultural development in the past half-century has been on a mechanistic basis: treating animals, soil and plants as if they were machines, and constantly tuning their performance to achieve higher yields. Agricultural research has all been directed towards the large farm: none has been seriously done to explore the performance possibilites, or improve the viability, of the smaller, or more mixed, farm. A simplified and less ecologically-rich countryside has been created in the process, particularly in the intensive arable lands of the eastern counties.

What seems so far to have escaped notice, however, is that what is happening to the countryside is not in any way extraordinary: it is exactly the same as has befallen the rest of society. Farmers have learnt to live like, and by the same rules as, the rest of us. They have moved into the twentieth century. And if we are going to demand that they revert to more humane, environment-sensitive working methods, the same responsibility has to be accepted, equally, by the urban population. The costs must be evenly spread across the whole community.

The fact that a wide section of the population enjoys some of the surplus produced by present business methods allows the majority to direct its disapproval purely at those near the top of the pyramid, and overlook the fact that they, its base, cover and are slowly abrading a large area of ground. Accomplices in the destruction of others' countries, or bribed and complaisantly acquiescing in that of our own, we are all responsible.

It is in the interests of privilege and the current centres of economic power that we should fail to address or understand these issues; to neglect the imperative to form a vision of the kind of world we want to live in, in spiritual, aesthetic or material terms. In a very true sense, the answer IS the question we have so far not systematically asked. A matter of being aware that there is something more than we have so far achieved, and being prepared to go and seek, and pay the costs for, it. In a word, things -including the environment - will have to be valued, not just on a market basis, but on a moral scale, and costed accordingly. Worldwide, such a revolution would require, for instance, that we open our ports to industrial goods from poorer economies than our own, and that we agree to pay prices for the raw materials and commodities we buy from them which reflect their cost of production, not just the balance of supply and demand.

Such a revolution is still probably remote: although there

are signs that the general public is beginning to be aware of its desirability. The revolution at home may be a rather closer prospect. For it is already clear that we cannot continue to pursue the agricultural methods we have used up till now without pushing environmental damage further than public opinion finds acceptable. Coercion and control in the countryside are not the answer: for they are as mechanistic as the methods they seek to manage. In any case, for the urban lobby to seek to impose them when it is its own demands that have led to the bad practices, is pure hypocrisy. What is required is nothing less than a complete change of heart and values.

At present, the countryside is occupied by several different groups, each pursuing its own self-interest under guise of a respectable falsehood: The gentrifiers - which includes both ex-urban investors in country property and the holders of great estates; the farmers, who say they are stewards, but are actually convinced exploiters; and conservationists, many of whom want to fossilise their particular dream and impose it on everyone else. What is needed is a new synthesis which re-establishes their interdependence.

We cannot stop the world and get off: a return to a de-industrialised William Morris world of crafts and organic foods is pure fantasy. However, a beginning can be made to reconstructing attitudes and activities. And that beginning will be made from the grass roots upwards. It will start by placing a proper emphasis back on the rural community, its life, its necessary infrastructure, its economic range and vigour. There is a basic human instinct, to husband and make the most of, a piece of territory we control. It displays itself both in the efficiency of the family-run farm and in the home-improving pride of the owner-occupier: but it is actually quite different from the empire-building gigantism which colonises and industrially organises thousand of acres. A secure tenant enjoying the respect of his landlord will invest in the improvement of his farm or home just as much as an owner. Jointly-owning housing co-operatives have produced as good aesthetic and social living conditions as private developments. What is important is that people should be able to exercise initiative and have control of their own fates: things which are just as much denied by bureaucratic council housing authorities that do not even allow tenants to choose their own colour schemes, or by rack-renting private landlords.

In agriculture, the imposition of pure business principles, while still allowing farmers to believe they are running their own enterprises, has narrowed their area of choice almost more than the most restrictive of landlords. The countryside has become, in many parts, a factory, and no one can live in a factory. In some parts, people who have gone to live in the country have started to demand that it cease to be a factory, and become instead a garden, a picture postcard or a museum. If that is what we want, then it will have to be paid for.

But the countryside we value is actually the product, not of planning, control or design: but of life and industry in the best sense; a rich tapestry woven by a multitude of different needs and activities. The factory is an over-simplification of those activities demanded by the laws of economics and the market. To restore the countryside, we have to moderate the power of those laws.

The last decade of the twentieth century offers a unique opportunity to do this: a real chance of replacing mono-product mass-production in the countryside with multi-activity richness, which can arrive at a living accommodation for the flux of population returning from the cities. It will involve reviving on a local scale some functions which transport and economies of scale have lately concentrated in towns; it will involve other things which have not before taken place in country settings. Home working, using modern communication techiques, clean light industry in relatively small workshops, and a whole range of social and service industries to enrich the life of countrydwellers and to cater for those who go there seeking recreation from the towns. And when this has grown up, the range of alternative and additional sources of income for members of the farm family will mean that agriculture itself can be conducted on other than a life-or-death industrial basis, for it will have become just one of a portfolio of enterprises: the backcloth, but by no means the whole of the countryside tapestry. The same people-centred approach is now the only sound basis for durable development anywhere.

But there is another step of understanding that also has to be taken in a densely-populated, urbanised country like Britain. That is to recognise that the nation's housing need has outgrown the outdated planning concept of town and country as separate entities. Even if only 1 per cent of the national housing stock is to be replaced each year, that will involve building 200,000 new homes annually - and the reduction in family size, with the increase in single and elderly people and single-parent families, makes that an increasingly pressing need. If we continue with a land market which allows the better-off to take it over at the expense of the less well-off, and to treat this private territory as something to be protected (via town and country planning) from development, new demands by the wealthy on a limited land area will raise prices near the main centres, and the inner city will remain deprived, demoralised and subject to terrorism - thus increasing the incentive for those who can afford to do so, to flee; and quite possibly in time leading to a reappearance of bandits preying on the wealthy rural areas too. Decent land in the city would become eroded, and the process of renewal become too expensive to undertake.

In this book I have tried to identify both the powers whose containment is essential if this new flowering is to take place; and the major constraints and forces which are conditions of the process in this country -the unavoidables. Once they are described and defined, some of the major areas can be seen where change and new growth can start; including, I hope, a realistic recognition that some activities will still have to be conducted on a scale which is worthy of the twentieth entury, which allows them still to be competitive and serve the needs of a large population. After all, 1 in 10 UK jobs are still agriculture-dependent: not just those working on-farm, but those manufacturing supplies for farmers, and processing, packing transporting and marketing their produce.

The 'forced march' of urbanisation and industrialisation - of which the growth of agribusiness is a significant part - has always taken place at the expense of the countryside. We need to find a way of minimising this cost without collapsing back into Luddite fantasies of a peasant agriculture. The relentless pressure of rising population and the advance of economic gigantism make it a difficult task. But it is a possibility. The seeds of environmental health, of a return of vigour to the countryside, lie in economic devolution: and that requires the reversal, not just of a few farming methods, but all of our assumptions.

BIBLIOGRAPHY

Andrae G. & Beckman B. : The Wheat Trap. Zed Books, 1985
Appleby M. : The Suffolk New Agricultural Landscapes Project. Suffolk C.C. 1986
Attwood E.A. : The Origins of State Support for British Agriculture. Manchester School Vol 31,2 May 1963 pp 129-48
Balasuriya T.: Planetary Theology. SCM Press 1984
Baldock D. & Conder D.: Can the CAP Fit the Environment? CPRE,1985
Barr C., Benefield C., Bunce R. : Landscape Changes in Britain. ITE, 1986
Berger J. : About Looking. Writers and Readers, 1980.
Body R. : Agriculture: the Triumph and the Shame. Temple Smith, 1982 Britton D.K. & Hill B.: Size and Efficiency in Farming. Saxon House 1979
Bowers J.K. : Do We Need More Forests? University of Leeds School of Economic Studies discussion paper No.137, 1986
Bowers J.K. & Cheshire P. : Agriculture, the Countryside and Land Use. Methuen, 1983.
Bull D. : A Growing Problem - Pesticides and the Third World Poor. Oxfam, 1982.
Carruthers S. P.: Alternative Enterprises for Agriculture in the UK. Centre for Agricultural Strategy, 1986
Coleman A. : Last Bid for Land-Use Sanity. Geographical Magazine, 1978, 50, 820-24
Coleman A. Utopia on Trial. Hilary Spurling, 1985
Cotgrove S. : Environmentalism and Utopia. Sociological Review, vol 24, No 1, February 1976 pp.23-42
Craig G. M., Jollans J. L., Korbey A.: The Case for Agriculture: and Independent Assessment. Centre for Agricultural Strategy, 1986
Darby H.C. : A Historical Geography of England before 1800. Cambridge, 1962.
Denman D.R.: Land Ownership and the Attraction of Capital into Agriculture: a British Overview. Land Economics 1965, 41, 209-16
Eade D. : An Unnatural Disaster: Drought in North-east Brazil. Oxfam 1985
Eversley D. : Conservation for the minority?. Built Environment,1974 Vol 3, January, pp 14-15
Foweraker J. : The Struggle for Land. Cambridge Latin American Studies, 1981
Harrison A.: Farmers and Farm Businesses in England. Reading University, 1975
Harrison F. : The Power in the Land: Unemployment, the profits crisis and the land speculator. Shepheard-Walwyn 1983
Harvey D. R., Barr C. J., Bell M., Bunce R. G. H., Edwards E., Errington A. J., Jollans J. L., McClintock J. H., Thompson A. .M M. & Tranter R. B. : Countryside Implications for England and Wales of possible changes in the Common Agricultural policy. Reading, Centre for Agricultural Strategy, 1986
Hill C.E. : The Future for Organically-grown Produce. Food From Britain, 1986
Holliday J. C.: Land at the Centre. Shepheard-Walwyn, 1986
Hoskins W.G.: The Making of the English Landscape. Hodder & Stoughton 1955
Ilbery B.W. : Agricultural Geography. Oxford University Press, 1985.
Jones E. L. & Mingay G. E., Land, Labour and Population in the Industrial Revolution. Edward Arnold, 1967
Korbey A.: Investing in Rural Harmony: a Critique. Centre for Agricultural Strategy, 1984
Korbey A.: Food Production and our Rural Environment: The Way Ahead. Centre for Agricultural Strategy, 1985
Korbey A. (Ed): Agriculture: the Triumph and the Shame. Centre for Agricultural Strategy, 1985
Lowe P., Cox G., MacEwen M., O'Riordan T., Winter M. : Countryside Conflicts.Gower/Temple Smith 1986

Lougheed J., Marsh J., Evans D., Rook J., Barber D., Dunning J., Mutch W.E.S., Wilkinson W., Watt, H. : Managing Change: Farming and the Countryside. FWAG,1986

Matthews A. : The Common Agricultural Policy and the Less-Developed Countries: Gill & Macmillan with Trocaire, 1985

Mingay G. E. : English Landed Society in the 18th Century. Routledge & Kegan Paul, 1963

Moyes A. : How Farming in Europe Affects the Third World Poor. Oxfam, 1986

Newby H., Bell C, Rose D., Saunders P. : Property, Paternalism and Power. Hutchinson, 1983

Norton-Taylor R. Whose Land Is It Anyway? : Turnstone Press, 1982

Taylor C. : Village & Farmstead. George Philip, 1984.

Rackham O.: Ancient Woodland. Edward Arnold, 1980

Ritson C.: Self-sufficiency and Food Security. Centre for Agricultural Strategy, 1980

Smith M.: Agricultura and Nature Conservation in Conflict - the Less-Favoured Areas of France and the UK. Arkleton Trust, 1985

Stinchcombe A. : Agricultural Enterprise and rural Class Relations. American Journal of sociology, Vol 67 No 2 pp.169-76

Tranter R. B.: Smallfarming and the Nation. Centre for Agricultural Strategy, 1980.

Twose N. : Why the Poor Suffer Most: Drought and the Sahel. Oxfam, 1986

Twose N. Cultivating Hunger. Oxfam, 1984

Whittemore C. : Land for People. Oxfam, 1981.

INDEX